The Expository Diamond

Four Steps to Relevant
Christ-Centered Preaching

Randy Rozelle

I often listen to great preaching with a mixture of admiration and disappointment. Some of the best preachers I have ever heard are so unique and so inimitable that, though one can appreciate their brilliance, their inscrutable methodology remains a profound mystery. On the other hand, some preaching that is faithful to the text is also so formulaic and homogeneous that, while it might be entirely decipherable, its repetitive and predictable structure is simply not very engaging. That's what makes *The Expository Diamond* such a homiletical jewel. Randy Rozelle offers a clear, reproducible methodology that exposits the text, engages the congregation, and spiritually matures the preacher while always seeking to exalt Christ.

> **Dr. Hershael W. York,** *The Southern Baptist Theological Seminary, Dean of the School of Theology; Victor and Louise Lester Professor of Christian Preaching, Louisville, Kentucky*

In this primer for preachers Randy Rozelle lays out the process for developing and delivering expository sermons in an engaging and accessible manner. His master image of a diamond—employed to envision this process—is apt and memorable. Rozelle's passion for preaching the riches of Scripture and especially the Gospel of Jesus Christ is evident in every chapter, and it infects the reader! This book uplifts and energizes fruitful biblical preaching.

> **Rev. Dr. David J. Peter,** *Professor of Practical Theology*
> *Concordia Seminary, St. Louis, Missouri*

Randy Rozelle puts Christ at the center of expository preaching, just as Christ is already at the center of Scripture. This Christological core sets this work off from much of the literature in contemporary homiletics. Placing Christ at the center of our preaching allows us to present truth in a person, crucial for today's hearers. After all, "Him we proclaim!" (Colossians 1:28). With one simple, creative metaphor after another, Rozelle provides the seminary student and working preacher with practical handles and best practices for the homiletical task.

> **Rev. Dr. Dean Nadasdy,** *President Emeritus*
> *Minnesota South District—LCMS*
> *Adjunct Professor, Homiletics, Concordia Seminary, St. Louis, Missouri*

The Expository Diamond will appeal to evangelical preachers—both new and seasoned. To make his point that expository preaching is a Christ-centered proclamation of a biblical passage's intended meaning that should transform lives, Rozelle draws upon the likes of Bryan Chapell, Fred Craddock, Tim Keller, Albert Mohler, and John Stott. Using the metaphor of a multi-faceted diamond, this book offers tried and tested homiletical advice that is eminently practical.

> **Rev. Dr. Reed Lessing,** *Senior Pastor*
> *St. Michael Lutheran Church, Fort Wayne, Indiana*

A good preacher takes deliberate steps to get himself out of the way in order to unleash the pure, unadulterated power of God's Word. He lets the biblical text dictate the sermon's central point, design, and homiletic strategies, always in relation to Christ's saving work. Good preaching applies that Word directly to real lives and real needs. Randy Rozelle offers urgent guidance to help the preacher uncover the glorious gem that is God's Word for all to see—a must-read for anyone who cares about the homiletic craft.
The Rev. Dr. A. Andrew Das, *Professor of Religious Studies and Assistant Dean of the Faculty*
Elmhurst College, Elmhurst, Illinois

All biblical interpretation is influenced by the preacher's own world view. Dr. Rozelle argues that a Christ-centered worldview should be the starting point for all expository preaching. He then provides an excellent and practical methodology in developing sermons that are faithful to the text, informed by the context, and applicable to the audience. I highly commend this book to all preachers, teachers, Bible study leaders, and anyone else who is charged with proclaiming God's Word.
Kevin Graham Ford, *Chief Catalyst*
Leighton Ford Ministries, Charlotte, North Carolina

If you are looking for a book that will challenge your thinking and provide practical insights to improve your preaching, *The Expository Diamond* is worth your time. Rozelle works to balance the necessary rigor of exegesis with the need for humility in the preacher, dependence upon God, along with the ultimate goal of piercing the heart and head of the hearer. There is no doubt you will find yourself inspired by Rozelle's passion for expository preaching.
Rev. Tim Niekerk, *Senior Pastor*
Salem Lutheran Church, Tomball, Texas

"Do you swear to tell the whole truth, and nothing but the truth?" is a common oath in courts of law. If this is the standard in the judicial realm, how much more so in the proclamation of God's Word within His Church? Expository preaching provides one of the most solid means to deliver the full veracity of the Bible to the hearer. Unfortunately, solid evangelical expository preaching that rightly divides the Word of Truth has gone out of fashion in much of the mainstream. Dr. Rozelle's *The Expository Diamond* can revive a dynamic and fulfilling homiletical approach by offering students and pastors a solid groundwork and methodology.
Dr. Chad Yeshayahu Foster, *Teaching Pastor*
St. Peter's Lutheran Church, Columbus, Indiana

If Christ-centered preaching is your aim, Rozelle's *The Expository Diamond* can be a helpful tool in hitting that mark. From offering a four-step process to sharing his personal passion, this book will help you discover and deliver the diamond-like brilliance that is God's Word.
Jon Peacock, *Lead Pastor*
Mission Church, Bloomingdale, Illinois

If God's people are, as Jesus implies, a treasure hidden that He sold all to buy, and if the preacher stands in the place of Jesus—an ambassador for Christ—it is the foolish preacher who sells his hearers short with lackluster messages offering self-help, sentiment, or satire rather than salvation. Randy Rozelle illuminates an easy to recall method by which every preacher can faithfully proclaim the Word of Christ that alone polishes His people and makes them shine! Faithful preaching requires diligence and effort, but if we believe Jesus, His people are worth that cost. For anyone who shares that task, this book is well worth it.
Mike Von Behren, *Pastor*
Holy Cross Lutheran Church, Spokane, Washington

Randy Rozelle has provided an extensive definition of expository preaching with a clear four-step discipline for sermon preparation. I appreciate his Christ-Centered emphasis and his use of practical application for the preacher. He provides helpful models to demonstrate his four steps.
The Rev. Dr. Larry Stoterau, *President Emeritus*
Pacific Southwest District, LCMS, Orange, California

Randy Rozelle provides a very helpful and practical book for practitioners of expository preaching. The concise, four-step process that comprises the expository diamond guides the preacher from text to proclamation in ways that are both faithful to the text and meaningful for the hearers. Above all else, I appreciate his emphasis upon the Christ-centered approach to Scripture and its exposition. This book would make an excellent textbook for the classroom as well as a source of growth for the seasoned pastor.
Rev. Dr. Glen Thomas, *Interim Senior Pastor*
St. Paul's Lutheran Church and School, St. Louis, Missouri

The Expository Diamond

Four Steps to Relevant Christ-Centered Preaching

Randy Rozelle

TENTH POWER

Elgin, IL · Tyler, TX

TENTHPOWERPUBLISHING
www.tenthpowerpublishing.com

Copyright © 2019 by Randy Rozelle

All rights reserved. No part of this book may be reproduced without permission from the author, except by a reviewer quoting brief passages in a review; nor may any part of this book be reproduced, stored in a retrieval system or copied by mechanical photocopying, recording or other means without written permission from the author.

Unless otherwise noted, Scripture quotations are from the ESV® Bible (The Holy Bible, English Standard Version®), copyright © 2001 by Crossway, a publishing ministry of Good News Publishers. Used by permission. All rights reserved.

Design by Inkwell Creative

Softcover ISBN 978-1-938840-29-6
e-book ISBN 978-1-938840-30-2

To my dear wife, Angie,
and to our children
Kayla, Ethan, and Adam:
Thank you for your patience
and support throughout this journey.
I love you more than you
will ever know.
Above all else in this life,
fight the good fight of THE FAITH:
keep those eyes locked on Jesus.

The *unfolding of Your words* gives light;
it imparts understanding to the simple.
–Psalm 119:130

TABLE OF CONTENTS

Preface 15

Chapter 1	A "Unique" Definition of Expository Preaching	17
Chapter 2	Ten Core (and Non-Negotiable) Tenets of Expository Preaching	23
Chapter 3	Introducing the Expository Diamond	47
Chapter 4	The Expository Diamond: Step Up	49
Chapter 5	The Expository Diamond: Step Back	53
Chapter 6	The Expository Diamond: Step Out	59
Chapter 7	The Expository Diamond: Step Forward	67
Chapter 8	The Expository Diamond: Expository Pitfalls	75
Chapter 9	Pull It Together: Destination Preaching and Sermon Structure	79
Chapter 10	Panning for Gold: Using Illustrations	91
Chapter 11	Top 10 Odds and Ends for Preaching	107
Chapter 12	Creative Expository Preaching: Sermons and Sermon Series	115
Chapter 13	Why Expository Preaching Matters: A Final Encouragement	131
Appendix A	Expository Sermon: Joshua 1:1-9	137
Appendix B	Expository Sermon: Luke 19:1-10	145
Appendix C	Sample Fill in the Blank Sermon Notes	153
Appendix D	Recommended Resources	155

Bibliography 159

PREFACE

I love preaching. In fact, I contend that preaching is the heartbeat of a congregation. Where preaching is prioritized, planned, prepared, and well-presented, the body of Christ pulsates with health, life, and growth—often numerically, always spiritually. However, where preaching is secondary, haphazard, or buried beneath a mound of other ministry tasks, the body of Christ limps forward—prone to routineness, stagnation, and even decline.

Therefore, whether you are new to preaching or a seasoned pastor who's visiting an old friend, I pray this book awakens or reaffirms your commitment to prioritize preaching in your ministry. This book is not intended to be an end-in-itself on the preparation of faithful expository sermons; rather, it functions as an *exceedingly practical*—even conversational—supplement to the other fine books in the field. Most chapters contain Scripture, wisdom from expositors, and recommended resources to assist your preaching ministry.

Remember, though, the best book on preaching is still your own Bible.

God's grace and blessing as you preach the Word!

Soli Deo Gloria

CHAPTER 1

A "Unique" Definition of Expository Preaching

If you are like me, you might be wondering, "What is expository preaching?" You ask a great question, and I do mean *question*. Although many preachers conceptually understand expository preaching and even practice it, surprisingly, a normative answer evades Christianity. Geologists and botanists do not share this conversation; no one questions or submits alternate definitions for *geology* or *botany*. On the contrary, even a brief exploration of contemporary books and publications on expository preaching reveals that no authoritative, universal definition exists; rather, subjectivity reigns. Prominent expositors in the field today offer variance in definition.

> Expository preaching is the communication of a biblical concept, derived from and transmitted through a historical, grammatical, and literary study of a passage in its context, which the Holy Spirit first applies to the personality and experience of the preacher, then through the preacher, applies to the hearers.[1]
>
> –Haddon Robinson

---

[1] Haddon Robinson, *Biblical Preaching: The Development and Delivery of Expository Messages*, 3rd ed. (Grand Rapids: Baker Book House, 2014), 5.

Expository preaching is the Spirit-empowered explanation and proclamation of the text of God's Word with due regard to the historical, contextual, grammatical, and doctrinal significance of the given passage, with the specific object of invoking a Christ-transforming response.[2]

–Stephen Olford and David Olford

An expository sermon may be defined as a message whose structure and thought are derived from a biblical text, that covers the scope of the text, and that explains the features and context of the text in order to disclose the enduring principles for faithful thinking, living and worship intended by the Spirit, who inspired the text.[3]

–Bryan Chapell

According to Webster, an exposition is a discourse to convey information or explain what is difficult to understand. Applying this idea to preaching requires that an expositor be one who explains Scripture by laying open the text to public view in order to set forth its meaning, explain what is difficult to understand, and make appropriate application... No matter what the length of the portion explained may be, if it is handled in such a way that its real and essential meaning as it existed in the mind of that particular Biblical writer and as it exists in the light of the overall context of Scripture is made plain and applied to the present-day needs of the hearers, it may properly be said to be *expository preaching*... In other words, expository preaching is Bible-centered preaching.[4]

–John MacArthur

Expository preaching is the process of laying open a biblical text in such a way that its original meaning is brought to bear on the lives

---

[2] Stephen F. Olford and David L. Olford, *Anointed Expository Preaching* (Nashville: Broadman & Holman Publishers, 1998), 69.

[3] Bryan Chapell, Christ-Centered Preaching: Redeeming the Expository Sermon, 2nd ed. (Grand Rapids: Baker Academic, 2005), 31

[4] John MacArthur, Jr., and The Master's Seminary Faculty, *Rediscovering Expository Preaching* (Dallas: Word Publishing, 1992), 11.

of contemporary listeners. And expository preaching is a discourse that expounds a passage of Scripture, organizes it around a central theme and main divisions which issue forth from the given text, and then decisively applies its message to the listeners.[5]

–Jerry Vines and Jim Shaddix

Expository preaching is the contemporization of the central proposition of a biblical text that is derived from the proper methods of interpretation and declared through effective means of communication to inform minds, instruct hearts, and influence behavior toward godliness.[6]

–Ramesh Richard

Expository preaching is that mode of Christian preaching that takes as its central purpose the presentation and application of the text of the Bible. All other issues and concerns are subordinate to the central task of presenting the biblical text. As the Word of God, the text of Scripture has the right to establish both the substance and the structure of the sermon.[7]

–R. Albert Mohler, Jr.

It is my contention that all true Christian preaching is expository preaching... Properly speaking, 'exposition' has a much broader meaning. It refers to the content of the sermon (biblical truth) rather than its style (a running commentary). To expound Scripture is to bring out of the text what is there and expose it to view. The expositor pries open what appears to be closed, makes plain what is obscure, unravels what is knotted and unfolds what is tightly packed. The opposite of exposition is "imposition," which is to impose on the text what is not there. But the "text" in question

---

[5] Jerry Vines and Jim Shaddix, *Power in the Pulpit: How to Prepare and Deliver Expository Sermons* (Chicago: Moody Press, 1999), 29.

[6] Ramesh Richard, *Preparing Expository Sermons: A Seven-Step Method for Biblical Preaching* (Grand Rapids: Baker Books, 2001), 19.

[7] R. Albert Mohler, Jr., *He Is Not Silent: Preaching in a Postmodern World* (Chicago: Moody Publishers, 2008), 65.

could be a verse, a sentence, or even a single word. It could equally be a paragraph, or a chapter, or a whole book. The size of the text is immaterial, so long as it is biblical. What matters is what we do with it. Whether it is long or short, our responsibility as expositors is to open it up in such a way that it speaks its message clearly, plainly, accurately, relevantly, without addition, subtraction or falsification.[8]

–John Stott

Expository preaching means text-driven.[9]

–T. J. Betts

Exposition means bringing out what is there. The word exposition derives from the Latin word *exposition*, which means "setting forth" or "making accessible." Therefore, an expository sermon is a sermon which faithfully brings a message out of Scripture and makes that message accessible to contemporary hearers.[10]

–*The Concise Encyclopedia of Preaching*

Given the plethora of definitions for expository preaching, Harold Bryson offers the following critique:

So many definitions of *expository preaching* have been developed through the years that writers on preaching have grouped the definitions into categories. Donald G. Miller gives four broad categories into which many definitions of expository preaching fall. Faris D. Whitesell establishes five broad categories of expository preaching... There is still no generally accepted definition of expository preaching. Many definitions have been constructed, but confusion still reigns.[11]

---

[8] John R. W. Stott, *Between Two Worlds: The Challenge of Preaching Today* (Grand Rapids: William B. Eerdmans Publishing Company, 1982), 126.

[9] Terry Betts, interview by author, Louisville, July 18, 2016.

[10] William H. Willimon and Richard Lischer, eds., *Concise Encyclopedia of Preaching* (Louisville: Westminster John Knox Press, 1995), 131.

[11] Harold T. Bryson, *Expository Preaching: The Art of Preaching through a Book of the Bible* (Nashville: Broadman & Holman Publishers, 1995), 12.

Bryson adds, "Each definition seems to be correct. Because of the variety of definitions, ambiguity abounds about a clear, authoritative, workable definition of expository preaching."[12]

To be sure, several similarities emerge from the aforementioned definitions, including (1) an adherence to the biblical text; (2) the concern for hearer application; and (3) the necessity of the Spirit's illumination. Nevertheless, one oversight stands out. Not one evangelical definition of expository preaching accentuates or even alludes to Christ-centered interpretation and proclamation of the preached text. If Christology is the cornerstone of Scripture and thus of faithful exposition too, how can Christological interpretation and proclamation be overlooked in definitions of expository preaching? Granted, Stephen Olford and David Olford include a "Christ-transforming response" in their definition, yet their definition still remains a far-cry from declaring Christ-centered exposition from text to hearer. Furthermore, given the explosion of religious pluralism in contemporary culture, it is too dangerous to assume Christocentricity in definitions and methodologies that do not forthright extol His hermeneutical Lordship over all Scripture. Otherwise, non-Christian religions that manipulate Scripture (i.e., Jehovah Witnesses, Mormons, etc.) could exploit the same definition.

Although Timothy Keller does not offer an explicit definition of expository preaching, his description nears Christocentricity:

> Expository preaching grounds the message in the text so that all the sermon's points are points in the text, and it majors in the text's major ideas. It aligns the interpretation of the text with the doctrinal truths of the rest of the Bible (being sensitive to systematic theology). And it always situates the passage within the Bible's narrative, showing how Christ is the final fulfillment of the text's theme (being sensitive to biblical theology).[13]

Notably, Keller's "definition" includes the textual, systematic, canonical, *and Christological* components of expository preaching. Moreover, as new definitions rush the homiletical field, hopefully

---

12 Ibid., 15.

13 Timothy Keller, *Preaching: Communicating Faith in an Age of Skepticism* (New York: Viking, 2015), 32.

Christological interpretation and proclamation of a passage's intended meaning push to the fore. To that end, I submit the following definition:

> *Expository preaching is the prayer-infused, Christ-centered interpretation and proclamation of a passage's intended meaning and purpose, which gives rise to Spirit-empowered application and implication in the lives of hearers today.*

God has laid the only expositional bridge from text to hearer, and that bridge is Christ.

CHAPTER 2

Ten Core (and Non-Negotiable) Tenets of Expository Preaching

In researching expository preaching, a significant question arose: Does expository preaching contain a set of core tenets that sermons must espouse to be rendered *expositional*, and if so, what are those tenets? The implications are profound. If a set of "expository essentials" exists then, subsequently, these components function as a norm by which the expository nature of all sermons can be gauged. Though some expositors might challenge this assertion, I believe that expository preaching stands on ten core tenets (or pillars). Not only do these "expository essentials" govern what necessitates expositional preaching in pulpits today, but, as a result, sermons that violate these fundamental principles on a consistent basis cannot be deemed *expository* by nature or by nurture.

Tenet 1: The Inerrancy of Scripture.
Scripture declares, "The word of the LORD proves true" (2 Sam 22:31). God Himself testifies, "I the LORD speak the truth; I declare what is right" (Isa 45:19). Jesus affirms in the priest-like prayer to His Father, "Sanctify them in the truth; Your word is truth" (John 17:17). Paul charges Timothy, "Do your best to present yourself to God as one approved, a worker who has no need to be ashamed; rightly handling the word of truth" (2 Tim 2:15). Paul later reiterates, "All Scripture is breathed out by God and profitable for teaching, for reproof, for

correction, and for training in righteousness" (2 Tim 3:16). Both Testaments maintain Scripture's inerrancy, inspiration, and infallibility.

Expository preaching, then, hinges on faith in Scripture's inerrancy—complete freedom from error and untruth. Without biblical inerrancy, preachers could not denounce sin on a weekly basis and summon scores, hundreds, even thousands of worshipers to repentance and faith in Jesus Christ. Furthermore, unless absolutely convinced that every word from Genesis to Revelation emanates from God, expositors could never speak with conviction the words that bear eternal ramification for every body and soul.

John MacArthur says,

> Evangelical preaching ought to reflect our conviction that God's Word is infallible and inerrant. Too often it does not. In fact, there is a discernable trend in contemporary evangelism *away* from biblical preaching and a drift *toward* experience-centered, pragmatic, topical approach in the pulpit. Should not our preaching be biblical exposition, reflecting our conviction that the Bible is the inspired, inerrant Word of God?[1]

Likewise, Jerry Vines and Jim Shaddix state, "The effective Bible expositor will have a high view of Scripture, beginning with a clear conviction about biblical *inspiration*."[2] Vines and Shaddix add, "A high view of biblical inspiration issues forth into a clear conviction regarding the Bible's *authority*. If the Bible is inspired by God and consequently void of error, then it can be trusted as the sole authority for matters of faith."[3] Thus, embracing complete biblical inerrancy, expositors preach what God has declared and willed to be written down, and they do so in the unwavering certitude that through *all* Scripture, God Himself continues to speak.

---

[1] John F. MacArthur and Masters Seminary Faculty, *Rediscovering Expository Preaching* (Dallas: Word Publishing, 1992), 23.

[2] Jerry Vines and Jim Shaddix, *Power in the Pulpit: How to Prepare and Deliver Expository Sermons* (Chicago: Moody Press, 1999), 49.

[3] Ibid., 53.

Tenet 2: Christ-Centered Interpretation and Proclamation.
Jesus gently—yet firmly—reprimands two disciples on the road to Emmaus: "'O foolish ones, and slow of heart to believe all that the prophets have spoken! Was it not necessary that the Christ should suffer these things and enter into his glory?' And beginning with Moses and all the Prophets, He interpreted to them in all the Scriptures the things concerning Himself" (Luke 24:25-27). Three times in three verses the word "all" distinguishes Jesus as *the Referent* of Scripture, a characteristic of Scripture that Jesus later speaks in the presence of all His disciples:

> These are My words that I spoke to you while I was still with you, that everything written about Me in the Law of Moses and the Prophets and the Psalms must be fulfilled... [I]t is written that the Christ should suffer and on the third day rise from the dead, and that repentance and forgiveness of sins should be proclaimed in His name to all nations, beginning from Jerusalem" (Luke 24:44-47).[4]

Jesus singularizes Himself as the interpretive key for Scripture. To miss Jesus as the fulcrum of biblical exposition, then, is to dismiss His hermeneutical blueprint for all of it.

The apostles exemplify Jesus's Christological hermeneutic in the New Testament church. Luke records, "And every day, in the temple and from house to house, they did not cease teaching and preaching Jesus as the Christ" (Acts 5:42). Likewise, Paul proclaims, "Jews demand signs and Greeks seek wisdom, but we preach Christ crucified, a stumbling block to Jews and folly to Gentiles" (1 Cor 1:22-23). Paul underscores a second time, "For I decided to know nothing among you except Jesus Christ and Him crucified" (1 Cor 2:2). Hence, Timothy Keller surmises, "For Paul ... there is only one topic: Jesus. Wherever we go in the Bible, Jesus is the main subject... So Paul hasn't preached unless he has preached about Jesus, not merely as an example to follow but as a savior: 'Christ Jesus, who has become for us our righteousness, holiness,

---

4 Cf. John 5:39, 46.

and redemption' (1 Cor 1:30)."[5] Paul knew no other interpretive lens for Scripture than Jesus of Golgotha.

It follows, then, that faithful expositors mirror Jesus's hermeneutic and apostolic example; they honor Christ as the focal point of biblical exposition. Dennis Cahill writes, "All Christian preaching should be gospel preaching. Not that all sermons are evangelistic or that all sermons should be based on New Testament texts, but all sermons should find their focus in the gospel, the story of the life, death, and resurrection of Jesus Christ."[6] Keller even bids preachers,

> Every time you expound a Bible text, you are not finished unless you demonstrate how it shows us that we cannot save ourselves and that only Jesus can. That means we must preach Christ from every text, which is the same as saying we must preach the gospel every time and not just settle for general inspiration or moralizing.[7]

Given Scripture's Christocentric nature, the homilist must decide how Christ impacts his respective text, and he must do this for every sermon.

Tenet 3: Grammatical-Historical Exegesis.

Divine decree necessitates textual integrity throughout the interpretive process. Paul instructs Timothy: "Do your best to present yourself to God as one approved, a worker who has no need to be ashamed, rightly handling the word of truth" (2 Tim 2:15). The Greek word for "rightly handling" (*orthotomeō*) means "to use correctly," "to teach aright," or "to expound correctly."[8] This holy directive is best accomplished through grammatical-historical exegesis. John Stott writes,

> *Exposition demands integrity...* It is sometimes graced with the rather long-winded adjective "grammatico-historical," because it signifies the interpretation of a text in accordance with both its

---

5 Timothy Keller, *Preaching: Communicating Faith in an Age of Skepticism* (New York: Viking, 2015), 16.

6 Dennis M. Cahill, *The Shape of Preaching* (Grand Rapids: Baker Books, 2007), 23.

7 Keller, *Preaching*, 48.

8 Walter Bauer, *A Greek-English Lexicon of the New Testament and Other Early Christian Literature*, rev. and ed. Frederick William Danker, 3rd ed. (Chicago: University of Chicago Press, 2000), 722.

historical origin and its grammatical construction. The sixteenth century Reformers are rightly given credit for having recovered this method by rescuing biblical interpretation from the fanciful allegorizations of medieval writers... They emphasize that what every Bible student must look for is the plain, natural, obvious meaning of each text, without subtleties. What did the original author intend his words to mean?[9]

Likewise, Walter Kaiser says, "The aim of the grammatico-historical method is to determine the sense [of the text] required by the laws of grammar and the facts of history."[10] Bryan Chapell also explains,

Our task as preachers is to discern what the original writers meant by analyzing the background and grammatical features of what they said. Using grammar and history to discern a text's original meaning is called the grammatical-historical method. This method allows Scripture to speak for itself instead of having an interpreter apply meaning to a text.[11]

Grammatical-historical exegesis pursues one hermeneutical goal: accuracy. Olford and Olford stress, "At the heart of expository preaching is a commitment to expose and proclaim the truth that is *there* in the text of God's Word. A primary and fundamental concern in sermon preparation is to discern accurately the truth that is really in the text."[12] Hence, expositors labor toward the literary, grammatical, contextual, historical, cultural, geographical, theological, and Christological accuracy of every passage. In this way, grammatical-historical exegesis demonstrates a preacher's commitment "to use correctly" the Word of truth.

---

9 John R. W. Stott, *Between Two Worlds: The Challenge of Preaching Today* (Grand Rapids: William B. Eerdmans Publishing Company, 1982), 127.
10 Walter C. Kaiser, Jr., *Toward an Exegetical Theology: Biblical Exegesis for Preaching & Teaching* (Grand Rapids: Baker Academic, 1981), 87.
11 Bryan Chapell, *Christ-Centered Preaching: Redeeming the Expository Sermon*, 2nd ed. (Grand Rapids: Baker Academic, 2005), 77.
12 Stephen F. Olford and David L. Olford, *Anointed Expository Preaching* (Nashville: Broadman & Holman Publishers, 1998), 102.

Tenet 4: One Governing Theme or Idea.
The magnitude of this tenet cannot be overstated. Haddon Robinson accentuates, "A sermon should be a bullet, and not buckshot. Ideally each sermon is the explanation, interpretation, or application of a single dominant idea supported by other ideas, all drawn from one passage or several passages of Scripture... Effective communication demands a single theme."[13] In fact, Robinson maintains that a preacher should never breach the pulpit until he can express the sermon's theme in a short, clear, and pregnant sentence.[14] Chapell concurs, "Without a unifying theme, listeners have no means of grasping a sermon's many thoughts."[15] Therefore, Chapell beseeches homilists: "*How many things is a sermon about? One!* ... Each feature of a well-wrought message reflects, refines, and/or develops one major idea ... all the features of a sermon should support the concept that unifies the whole."[16] Furthermore, because hearers cannot pause live sermons nor press "rewind," Chapell reminds clergy that "sermons are for listeners, not readers... It is easier to catch a baseball [i.e., one homiletical theme] than a handful of sand even if the two weigh about the same."[17]

To underscore the importance of a unifying homiletical theme, Fred Craddock utilizes a water analogy:

> The difference between a moving stream and a stagnant marsh is constraint. Such is the difference between sermons with and without the discipline of the controlling theme... If there is not a single theme, all the energies that should have been harnessed to the one task are scattered and dispersed in the frantic search for a place to stop that will give the semblance of planning to this aimless wandering.[18]

Craddock even provides a litmus test to ensure cohesive sermonic

---

13 Haddon Robinson, *Biblical Preaching: The Development and Delivery of Expository Messages,* 3rd ed. (Grand Rapids: Baker Book House, 2014), 17.
14 Ibid., 18.
15 Chapel, *Christ-Centered Preaching,* 43.
16 Ibid., 44.
17 Ibid., 43.
18 Fred Craddock, *As One without Authority* (St. Louis: Chalice Press, 2001), 82.

themes: "All this has been to say again that unity is difficult to achieve but irreplaceable if the sermon is to move... The desired unity has been gained when the preacher can state the central germinal idea in one simple affirmative sentence."[19]

It is imperative, however, for the text to govern the unifying theme. John MacArthur clarifies, "The central idea of a true expository message reflects the central idea intended by the Bible author himself... Our task is NOT to create a central theme. It is rather to 1. Find the author's central theme, 2. Build a message around that theme, and 3. Make that theme the central part of all we have to say."[20] Likewise, Chapell states, "In expository preaching, unity occurs when a preacher demonstrates that the elements of a passage support a single major idea, which serves as the theme of the sermon. We want this theme to be the Bible's theme."[21] In addition, John Broadus writes,

> What now is the prime requisite to the effectiveness of an expository sermon? Our answer must be, unity. Unity in a discourse is necessary to instruction, to conviction, and to persuasion ... but unity in an expository discourse is by many preachers never aimed at. They conceive of it as a mere series of disjointed remarks upon the successive verses... Let there be unity at whatever cost. And not only this, but structure.[22]

Without a central theme, controlling idea, or governing image, preachers are prone to "pinball preaching." In pinball preaching, a sermon launches from the pulpit in one direction, then abruptly shifts to one or more subsequent directions. A sermon goes here; then a sermon goes there. Suddenly, out of nowhere, the sermon returns to a previous point. *AAAHHH!* Fatigued from trying to follow along, the hearers rejoice when at last—and likely long-past!—the homily is "GAME OVER."

---

19 Ibid., 85.
20 MacArthur, *Rediscovering Expository Preaching*, 229.
21 Chapell, *Christ-Centered Preaching*, 46.
22 John A. Broadus, *A Treatise on the Preparation and Delivery of Sermons* (Philadelphia: Smith, English & CO., 1871), 304-5. Bryan Chapell actually dubs John Broadus "the father of modern expository preaching" (*Christ-Centered Preaching*, 85).

Tenet 5: An Advantageous Structure.
David Helm acknowledges, "Each week the preacher faces a ... challenge: How should I arrange the material I intend to preach? What organization will I bring to it?"[23] Helm's admission undoubtedly resonates with expositors. The text has been quarried, the central idea has been gleaned, and the intention of the passage and sermon has been clearly stated. Now, the homilist must organize the blossoming message for maximum flow, interest, unity, and comprehension. While the goal of grammatical-historical exegesis is accuracy, the goal of sermon structure is cohesive progression. Keller says, "Your outline has to have movement, progression, tension... In your sermons you must build some suspense that creates an eagerness to hear what is coming next and a sense of traveling to a destination."[24]

For the sake of homiletical progression, Chapell advises preachers: "A well-planned sermon begins with a good outline—a logical path for the mind... Good outlines clarify the parts and progress of a sermon in listeners' minds."[25] Chapell adds, "The goal of good outlining is to make sure listeners can follow a sermon's thought, not reproduce a preacher's outline."[26] Accordingly, Chapell accentuates the importance of a sermon's framework including three parts—an introduction, a body, and a conclusion:

> Sermons typically begin with an introduction that leads to a proposition that indicates what the body of the sermon will discuss. The body includes main points and subpoints that form the skeletal outline of the sermon and structure the sermon's explanation. The explanatory materials, which support the main and subpoint statements, as well as the sermon's illustrations and applications flesh out the skeleton formed by the explanation's points. A conclusion follows the body of the message, summarizing the information in the message and usually containing the sermon's

---

23 David R. Helm, *Expositional Preaching: How We Speak God's Word Today* (Wheaton, IL: Crossway, 2014), 97.

24 Keller, *Preaching*, 228. For an insightful resource about the sermon as a journey toward a destination, see Andy Stanley and Lane Jones, *Communicating for a Change* (Sisters, OR: Multnomah Publishers, 2006).

25 Chapell, *Christ-Centered Preaching*, 133.

26 Ibid., 135.

most powerful appeal.[27]

Moreover, in light of contemporary Western culture, MacArthur insists that introductions, main points, and conclusions need to be well-crafted:

> If a preacher fails to gain his audience's attention with a captivating introduction, he has probably lost them for the rest of the message. If his main points are not clarified or made memorable with quality illustrations, then the effect of his message can be short-lived. If he bypasses concluding his remarks with a review or exhortation, the purpose of the message will probably not be achieved.[28]

Although expositors agree on the importance of sermon outlines for effective preaching, they disagree on the nature of those structures. As a result, two primary camps have emerged within modern expository preaching. One camp endorses "open-structure" exposition, while the other camp adheres to "closed-structure" exposition. *Open-structure* exposition maintains that while the text must guide the homiletical outline, the text does not bind the sermon to a specific structure. Rather, the expositor is free to choose a structure that best communicates the intended purpose of the text. Conversely, *closed-structure* exposition demands that sermon structures adhere to the structure of the text itself.

Respectable preachers appear in both camps. For instance, David Helm and R. Albert Mohler, Jr. maintain a closed-structure approach to exposition. Helm says,

> We don't superimpose our outline over the text. Rather, we bring out of the text what the Holy Spirit already put in. And this is best done in the manner in which he put it together... I have defined biblical exposition as empowered preaching that rightly submits the shape and emphasis of the sermon to the shape and emphasis of a biblical text.[29]

---

27 Chapell, *Christ-Centered Preaching*, 135.
28 MacArthur, *Rediscovering Expository Preaching*, 243.
29 Helm, *Expositional Preaching*, 101.

Mohler even challenges, "If you picked an evangelical church at random and attended a Sunday morning service there, how likely is it that you would hear a faithful expository sermon, one that takes its message and its structure from the biblical text?"[30] Mohler therefore insists,

> Because the Bible is the inerrant and infallible Word of God, the very shape of the biblical text is also divinely determined. God has spoken through the inspired human authors of Scripture, and each different genre of biblical literature—historical narrative, direct discourse, and apocalyptic symbolism, among others—demands that the preacher give careful attention to the structure of the text and allow it to shape the sermon… But genuine exposition demands that the text establish the shape as well as the substance of the sermon.[31]

Thus, with closed-structure exposition, the shape and substance of the sermon *must derive* from the shape and substance of the text.

On the other hand, Harold Bryson and Timothy Keller embrace an open-structure approach to exposition. Bryson states,

> The form for sermons has never been fixed, nor will it ever be fixed. The *message* of preaching is far more important than the *method* of preaching. God uses many kinds of expositors to present his Word… Some expositors employ a didactic offering while others utilize an inductive or narrative approach. Preachers select and arrange words in a sermon differently. They organize their thoughts with structural diversity. No one style of preacher and no one kind of sermon characterizes the preaching of the Word. A sermon is authentic when it brings the truth of a text in touch with contemporary needs. The issue in a sermon is not *how* God's truth is exposed but *if* God's truth is exposed. Biblical truth in a sermon can be exposed either explicitly with a deductive approach or implicitly with an inductive approach. *The manner*

---

[30] R. Albert Mohler, Jr., *He Is Not Silent: Preaching in a Postmodern World* (Chicago: Moody Publishers, 2008), 50.

[31] Ibid., 67.

does not matter but the message does.[32]

Likewise, Keller maintains, "Once you have chosen the theme, develop an *outline* around that theme that unfolds the meaning of the passage—with each point arising from insights from the text itself—and creates narrative tension toward a climax."[33] While Bryson and Keller affirm that a sermon structure must draw from the text itself, they do not stipulate that their structures coincide.

Lest the task of sermon structure becomes legalistic and restrictive, open-structure exposition is preferred. The Holy Spirit not only endows preachers with creativity, but pastors exercise the freedom of the gospel in sermon design. After all, sermon structure—though indispensable—is neither commanded nor forbidden in Scripture (i.e., adiaphora) and thereby left to the prayerful discretion of the homilist. While a sermon outline may reflect the exact layout of a text, such alignment is not required to faithfully expound Holy Writ.

Tenet 6: The Proper Distinction between Law and Gospel.
Although the proper distinction between law and gospel could be placed under theological accuracy, the distinction deserves its own tenet of expository preaching. Contrary to the assumption that the First Testament is *law* (i.e., the wrathful, Old Testament God) and the Second Testament is *gospel* (the loving Jesus), both Testaments contain law and gospel. In fact, the Bible commences with pure gospel: God summons a universe (*ex nihilo*) into existence with a planet that He orders to support created life (Gen 1). In Genesis 2, God builds (*banah*) a wife—a suitable helper—and "walks her down the aisle" to the man (v. 22).[34]

---

[32] Harold T. Bryson, *Expository Preaching: The Art of Preaching through a Book of the Bible* (Nashville: Broadman & Holman Publishers, 1995), 7-8.

[33] Keller, *Christ-Centered Preaching*, 225.

[34] Psalm 127:1 uses the same word for God: "Unless the LORD builds (*banah*) the house, those who build it labor in vain." From the very beginning, we have a God who loves to build with His hands. Is there any wonder, then, that of all the possible occupations for Jesus, Mark 6:3 says, "Is not this *the carpenter*, the Son of Mary and brother of James and Joses and Judas and Simon? And are not His sisters here with us?" Both testaments feature the same God. Hence, it is no surprise when Jesus says: "In My Father's house are many rooms ... I go to prepare a place for you" (John 14:2). What is Jesus, the Carpenter-God, doing now? Precisely what God has been doing since Genesis 1: He continues to build!

Imagine the smile on God's face, and Adam's! In Genesis 3, though God pronounces dire judgment on mankind for his disobedience and fall into sin (law), God promises a Seed (*zera'*) who will deal a decisive blow to the serpent's head (gospel). God even clothes Adam and Eve (i.e., gospel) after their realized nudity (Gen 3:21).[35] In the Second Testament, passages such as Romans 6:23 contain *both* law and gospel: "For the wages of sin is death (law), but the free gift of God is eternal life in Christ Jesus our Lord (gospel)." Hence, rightly dividing law and gospel becomes a prerequisite for the faithful exposition of both Testaments.

In short, the law shows human sin, and the gospel shows humanity's Savior. Martin Luther writes,

> The Law is the Word in which God teaches and tells us what we are to do and not to do, as in the Ten Commandments... And so the Law of God convinces us by our experience that we are naturally wicked, disobedient, lovers of sins, and enemies of God's Commandments... The other Word of God is not Law or commandment, nor does it require anything of us; but after the first Word, that of the Law, has done this work and distressful misery and poverty have been produced in the heart, God comes and offers His lovely, living Word, and promises, pledges, and obligates Himself to give grace and help, that we may get out of this misery and that all sins not only be forgiven but also blotted out and that love and delight to fulfill the Law may be given besides. See, this divine promise of His grace and of the forgiveness of sins is properly called Gospel.[36]

Luther's successors further explain:

> We believe, teach, and confess that the law is, strictly speaking, a

---

35 Not only does God make (*'asah*) the first clothes (lit. tunics or garments) in world history (i.e., Made in Eden), but in doing so, God takes the first animal life (lit. skins). In other words, the LORD provides the sacrifice to clothe His sinful children, meaning God shed the first and the last sacrificial blood in Scripture (cf., 1 Cor 5:7; Heb 9:26). The latter, of course, is "the Lamb of God, who takes away the sin of the world" (John 1:29; cf., Heb 9:14); He clothes sinful man with His righteousness now and for eternity (cf., Gal 3:27; Rev 7:9, 13).

36 Ewald M. Plass, comp., *What Luther Says: A Practical In-Home Anthology for Active Christians* (St. Louis: Concordia Publishing House, 1959), 735.

divine teaching which gives instruction regarding what is right and God-pleasing and condemns everything that is sin and contrary to God's will... However, the gospel is, strictly speaking, the kind of teaching that reveals ... that Christ has atoned and paid for all sins and apart from any human merit has obtained and won for people the forgiveness of sins ... and eternal life.[37]

Rightly dividing law and gospel in preaching amounts to hearers being uncertain or confident of their salvation, fearful or comforted, weak or strong, doubtful or joyful, captive or victorious in Christ. To only preach God's law leaves hearers down trodden and terrified by sin, guilt, and eternal condemnation. Yet, to only preach the gospel (narrow sense) cheapens the gifts of forgiveness and eternal life that Jesus purchased at His life's expense. Moreover, without law proclamation, sinful man feels no urgency or dire need for Christ; and without gospel proclamation, contrite sinners do not hear of God's comprehensive coverage plan (i.e., complete forgiveness) in Christ. Therefore, the Lutheran confessors state,

The distinction between law and gospel is a particularly glorious light. It serves to divide God's Word properly [cf. 2 Tim 2:15] and to explain correctly and make understandable the writings of the holy prophets and apostles. Therefore, we must diligently preserve this distinction, so as not to mix these two teachings together and make the gospel into a law. For this obscures the merit of Christ and robs troubled consciences of the comfort that they otherwise have in the holy gospel when it is preached clearly and purely.[38]

As a result, the proper distinction between law and gospel is crucial to exposition, especially given the number of consciences that God entrusts to a pastor's homiletical care.

When distinguishing law and gospel, however, preachers must guard against "auto mode." In "auto mode," homilists force the dual hermeneutic (i.e., both law and gospel) onto every passage of Scripture,

---

37 Robert Kolb and Timothy J. Wengert, eds., *The Book of Concord: The Confessions of the Evangelical Lutheran Church* (Minneapolis: Fortress Press, 2000), 500.

38 Kolb and Wengert, *The Book of Concord*, 581.

or, by default, they read law and gospel *into* every text. Instead, expositors should draw out of a text only what it contains, be it law, gospel, or both. To take a case in point, a pastor started a sermon on Matthew 14:13-21 by asking, "Where is the law here?" (a rather dull introduction too.) A few minutes later he asked, "And where is the gospel here?"—the classic law-gospel sermon structure. Although his intention (and sermon) was orthodox, this text does not contain law per se; rather, it demonstrates the goodness and divinity of Jesus (gospel). Granted, law and/or gospel can be brought into proclamation via a passage's larger context and biblical theology, but in this particular passage, the pastor tried to siphon law where there was only gospel.

Tenet 7: Application and Implication.
Haddon Robinson asserts,

> Application gives expository preaching purpose. As shepherds we relate to the hurts, cries, and fears of our flock... [T]hey lie awake wondering about grocery prices, crop failures, quarrels with a spouse, diagnosis of a malignancy, a frustrating sex life, or the rat race where only rats seem to win... [W]e exegete both the Scripture and the congregation.[39]

Exposition without application might inform a congregation, but it will not guide, motivate, challenge, or produce life change in them. Bryan Chapell explains, "So what? What do you want me to do or believe? If you cannot answer, you have not preached... The healthiest preaching does not assume listeners will automatically see how to apply God's truths to their lives; it supplies the application people need."[40] Chapell adds, "Expository preaching does not merely obligate preachers to explain what the Bible says; it obligates them to explain what the Bible means in the lives of people today. Application is as necessary for sound exposition as is explication."[41] Similarly, John Broadus says, "Application in a sermon is not merely an appendage to the discussion,

---

[39] Robinson, *Biblical Preaching*, 10.
[40] Chapell, *Christ-Centered Preaching*, 53.
[41] Ibid., 84.

or a subordinate part of it, but is the main thing to be done... We are not to speak *before* the people, but *to* them, and must earnestly strive to make them take what we say to themselves."[42] Application links the text to present-day hearers. Application answers questions such as, "How does this unchanging truth of God's Word apply to contemporary culture? Why is this passage important to me? How does this text speak to my life today?"

Chapell uses a baseball analogy to underscore the importance of application in preaching:

> Without application, a preacher simply swings blindly, hoping that the ball of application will hit the bat of exposition. Home runs are more frequently hit when the batter sees the ball before swinging... Preachers should exegete a text *and* their congregation to decide the response they intend before they craft the words of the sermon.[43]

At the same time, however, Mohler cautions expositors regarding the two extremes of application:

> Application is absolutely necessary, but it is also fraught with danger. Haddon Robinson describes the "heresy of application," warning that many preachers are faithful in the task of exegesis, but undermine the text at the point of application. At the other extreme are preachers who never get to the task of application at all, arguing that application is an attempt to do the work of the Holy Spirit... [T]he faithful preacher understands the difference between the external application of the text to life and the Spirit's internal application of the Word to the heart.[44]

Textual application, then, must reside in the power of the gospel. David Helm reminds preachers, "A final check on my work is to ask a question that points me back to the heart of the Bible itself. Is the

---

42 Broadus, *A Treatise on the Preparation and Delivery of Sermons*, 230.
43 Chapell, *Christ-Centered Preaching*, 213.
44 Mohler, *He Is Not Silent*, 68.

application I am making grounded in the gospel, or am I in danger of simply placing more commands on my people?"[45] Only the gospel's power can effect life change in hearers as the text is applied to the gathered.

Nehemiah 8 exemplifies hearer application. Ezra, the priest and scribe, stands at a podium before the people of Israel and reads the Torah from morning to midday. The text notes that a company of Levites "causes the people to have understanding with respect to the Torah" (v. 7, author's translation). In fact, the Levites give such clarity of the text to Israel (i.e., application) that the people begin to weep and mourn (vv. 8-9). The gravity of the people's response demonstrates why exposition requires application: because application both *individualizes* and *personalizes* Scripture for its hearers.

Furthermore, gospel-driven application always produces Spirit-empowered implication. While application answers the "So what?" of a passage, implication unfolds the "Now what?" of a text. Implication, then, drives home the intended purpose of the text and sermon. Robinson explains,

> The purpose states what you expect to happen in your hearers as a result of preaching your sermon… Whole books, as well as sections within books, were written to make something happen in the thinking and the actions of the readers… You must first figure out why a particular passage was included in the Bible, and with this in mind decide what God desires to accomplish through your sermon in your hearers today.[46]

Likewise, Vines and Shaddix instruct,

> Every message ought to have a specific purpose aimed at a particular group of people. This purpose defines what you want the audience to take away with them—what you want them to do… The purpose of your message is what you desire in terms of audience response. You know what the sermon is about, including

---

45 Helm, *Expositional Preaching*, 109.
46 Robinson, *Biblical Preaching*, 73.

its central thrust... What do you want your listeners *to do* about that subject?⁴⁷

Hence, Ramesh Richard states, "By the end of the sermon the audience must have the answers to three important questions: [1] *What* did the preacher speak about? [2] *So what* difference does or should it make? [3] *Now what* do I do with God's claims in this sermon?"⁴⁸ Richard's second question ensures hearer application, while his third question spotlights textual implication.

The Bible demonstrates textual implication from week one. On day 6 of Creation, God's first ever words to Adam and Eve are to "be fruitful and multiply and fill the earth and subdue it and have dominion over the fish of the sea and over the birds of the heavens and over every living thing that moves on the earth" (Gen 1:28). The textual implications for husband and wife are to (1) enjoy frequent sexual union, resulting in procreation; and to (2) steward the animal kingdom. In other words, God says (loose translation), "I have given you life, marital union, and this bountiful new earth. Thrive in the relationships (vertical and horizontal) that I have designed for your well-being." Furthermore, because God does not change, the Holy Spirit continues to direct and empower textual application and implication in hearers until Christ's return (see Ezek 36:27; Gal 5:16).

Tenet 8: Divine Dependence.
Jesus promises His disciples, "I will ask the Father, and He will give you another Helper, to be with you forever, even the Spirit of truth... He dwells with you and will be in you... He will teach you all things and bring to your remembrance all that I have said to you" (John 14:16-17, 26). Jesus restates that very evening,

> It is to your advantage that I go away, for if I do not go away, the Helper will not come to you. But if I go, I will send Him to you... When the Spirit of truth comes, He will guide you into all the truth, for He will not speak on His own authority, but whatever

---

47 Vines and Shaddix, *Power in the Pulpit*, 137.
48 Ramesh Richard, *Preparing Expository Sermons: A Seven-Step Method for Biblical Preaching* (Grand Rapids: Baker Books, 2001), 117.

He hears He will speak, and He will declare to you the things that are to come. He will glorify Me, for He will take what is Mine and declare it to you. All that the Father has is Mine; therefore I said that He will take what is mine and declare it to you. (John 16:7-15)

In Christ, all of God's promises are *yes* (2 Cor 1:20). Ten days after Jesus ascends to the Father's right hand, Jesus bequeaths His church with the Holy Spirit. Pentecost means that the church now exegetes and expounds Scripture in the power and illumination of the Holy Spirit. As a result, the entire expository process depends upon the presence and aid of God's Divine Tutor.

Charles Spurgeon likens a preacher's divine dependence to a dormant church bell:

> The preacher, no matter how brilliant, godly, or eloquent, has no power without the Spirit's help: The bell in the steeple may be well hung, fairly fashioned, and of soundest metal, but it is dumb until the ringer makes it speak. And ... the preacher has no voice of quickening for the dead in sin, or of comfort for living saints unless the divine spirit [Spirit] gives him a gracious pull, and begs him speak with power.[49]

Similarly, Olford and Olford acknowledge, "The preacher must depend upon the aid and the anointing of the Holy Spirit as he preaches the Word. Such prayer and dependence is not an excuse for sloppy preparation. Indeed, the preacher should have been dependent on the Holy Spirit in the study as well."[50] Vines and Shaddix concur:

> The expository preacher has a powerful ally as he seeks creatively to communicate God's Word to the person in the pew. He has been promised the assistance of the Holy Spirit... The Spirit can arouse in the hearers deep desires to know the truth. He has been given by our Lord to bring men to an awareness of their sinfulness, the

---

[49] Charles H. Spurgeon, *The Quotable Spurgeon* (Wheaton, IL: Harold Shaw, 1990), 207, quoted in MacArthur, *Rediscovering Expository Preaching*, 83.

[50] Olford and Olford, *Anointed Expository Preaching*, 180.

adequacy of the work of Christ, and the desirability of salvation through Him. The power of the Holy Spirit makes preaching effective and applicable. Paul stated in 1 Thess. 1:5, "For our gospel did not come to you in word only, but also in power, and in the Holy Spirit and in much assurance."[51]

Preachers best express their dependence on the Spirit's power and illumination through prayer. Not surprisingly, prayer brackets Jesus's promise of the Holy Spirit in John 14–16. Before Jesus promises the Helper in John 14:16-17, He pledges, "Whatever you ask in My name, this I will do, that the Father may be glorified in the Son. If you ask Me anything in My name, I will do it" (vv. 13-14). In the same way, after Jesus promises the Helper's assistance in John 16:13-15, He reiterates: "In that day you will ask nothing of Me. Truly, truly, I say to you, whatever you ask of the Father in My name, He will give it to you. Until now you have asked nothing in My name. Ask, and you will receive, that your joy may be full" (vv. 23-24). Hence, prayer bookends the promise of the Spirit's guidance into all biblical truth.

Expositors therefore lean on the Holy Spirit and pray from the study to the pulpit. Dennis Cahill writes,

> The preacher can at least be aware of the need for the Spirit's help in all phases of the sermon design... We should begin the sermon development process with focused prayer, inviting the Spirit of God into the sermon design process. Along the way we will often pray short prayers, asking for God's help. And we will conclude, not just with a sense of relief, but with a prayer of thanksgiving for the Spirit's involvement.[52]

David Helm also acknowledges, "In a word, we are desperate—desperate for the power of the Holy Spirit to attend our preaching. And so we pray. We pray in advance of preaching. We pray in the act of preaching. We pray even after our preaching is done."[53] Not only

---

51 Vines and Shaddix, *Power in the Pulpit*, 189.
52 Cahill, *The Shape of Preaching*, 88.
53 Helm, *Expositional Preaching*, 91.

does Christ's promise of the Spirit's assistance inspire pastors to bathe the entire homiletical journey in prayer, but His promise convicts clergy for those times when they have allowed competing ministry demands to shelve the power and results that accompany prayer-soaked sermons.

Tenet 9: Complementing Character.
Although God *equips the called* rather than *calling the equipped*, Scripture reveals that God regards the character of His servants.[54] Accordingly, God lists several requirements for men who desire to oversee His flock. Paul instructs Timothy:

> If any aspires to the office of overseer, he desires a noble task. Therefore an overseer must be above reproach, the husband of one wife, sober-minded, self-controlled, respectable, hospitable, able to teach, not a drunkard, not violent but gentle, not quarrelsome, not a lover of money. He must manage his own household well, with all dignity keep his children submissive, for if someone does not know how to manage his own household, how will he care for God's church? He must not be a recent convert, or he may become puffed up with conceit and fall into the condemnation of the devil. Moreover, he must be well thought of by outsiders, so that he may not fall into disgrace, into a snare of the devil (1 Tim 3:1-7).

Paul also directs Titus:

> This is why I left you in Crete, so that you might put what remained into order, and appoint elders in every town as I directed you—if anyone is above reproach, the husband of one wife, and his children are believers and not open to the charge of debauchery or insubordination. For an overseer, as God's steward, must be above reproach. He must not be arrogant or quick-tempered or a drunkard or violent or greedy for gain, but hospitable, a lover of good, self-controlled, upright, holy, and disciplined. He must hold firm to the trustworthy word as taught, so that he may be able to

---

54 Zechariah and Elizabeth (Luke 1:6); Joseph (Matt 1:19); Mary (Luke 1:38); Anna (Luke 2:36-38); the women who accompany Jesus (Luke 8:1-3); the seven assistants (Acts 6:3); Stephen (Acts 6:8), deacons (1 Tim 3:8-13), et al.

give instruction in sound doctrine and also to rebuke those who contradict it (Titus 1:5-9).

If a gap exists between the sermon and the life of the preacher, the message of Christ lacks credibility to its hearers. Accordingly, several expositors reflect on the importance of a preacher's character. Broadus states, "Nor must we ever forget the power of character and life to reinforce speech. What a preacher *is*, goes far to determine the effect of what he says."[55] Similarly, John MacArthur says, "If the life of the preacher does not harmonize with his words, the resultant discord will drown out the message, regardless of how well prepared and delivered it is... Ultimately ... our sermons will only be as persuasive as our lives."[56] Granted, a pastor's character hinges on God's grace in Jesus to battle his own sinfulness; however, he must actively strive by the indwelling of the Holy Spirit to reflect God's standards for ministry in his personal, familial, congregational, and communal life. To behave otherwise disdains the office and discredits the message of the gospel. Let the church, then, plead for her pastors: "Gracious Lord, keep all who bear the yoke of the pastoral office from behaviors that hinder gospel receptivity. In Jesus's name. Amen."

Tenet 10: Hard Work.
God so reveres the toil of preaching that He bids the church through the apostle Paul: "Let the elders who rule well be considered worthy of double honor, especially those who *labor in preaching and teaching*. For the Scripture says, 'You shall not muzzle an ox when it treads out the grain,' and, 'The laborer deserves his wages'" (1 Tim 5:17-18). In verse 17, the Greek verb *kopiaō* means "to toil," "to grow tired," or "to be weary"; such toil includes physical, mental, and spiritual exertion.[57] In other words, *kopiaō* implies that expository preaching comes at a price; namely, that of extensive labor.

Thus, John Broadus asserts,

---

55 Broadus, *A Treatise on the Preparation and Delivery of Sermons*, 504.
56 MacArthur, *Rediscovering Expository Preaching*, 327, 345.
57 Bauer, *A Greek-English Lexicon*, 558.

If the suggestions which have been offered are well-founded, it will be obvious that expository preaching is a difficult task. It requires much close study of Scripture in general, and much special study of the particular passage to be treated. To make a discourse which shall be explanatory and yet truly oratorical, bearing a rich mass of details but not burdened with them, full of Scripture and abounding in practical applications, to bring even dull, uninformed and unspiritual minds into interested and profitable contact with an extended portion of the Bible—of course this must be difficult.[58]

Timothy Keller agrees,

Understanding the biblical text, distilling a clear outline and theme, developing a persuasive argument, enriching it with poignant illustrations, metaphors, and practical examples, incisively analyzing heart motives and cultural assumptions, making specific application to real life—all of this takes extensive labor.[59]

In fact, Jay Adams even associates poor preaching with inadequate sermon preparation:

My point is that good preaching demands hard work. From listening to sermons and from talking to hundreds of preachers about preaching, I am convinced that the basic reason for poor preaching is the failure to spend adequate time and energy in preparation. Many preachers—perhaps most—simply don't work long enough on their sermons.[60]

Mohler therefore renounces any shortcuts to expository preaching:

Expository preaching is therefore inescapably bound to the serious work of exegesis. If the preacher is to explain the text, he must first

---

[58] Broadus, *A Treatise on the Preparation and Delivery of Sermons*, 317-18.

[59] Keller, *Preaching*, 11.

[60] Jay E. Adams, "Editorial: Good Preaching is Hard Work," *The Journal of Pastoral Practice* 4, no. 2 (1980): 1, as quoted by MacArthur, *Rediscovering Expository Preaching*, 210.

study the text and devote the hours of study and research necessary to understand it. The pastor must invest the largest portion of his energy and intellectual engagement (not to mention his time) to this task of "accurately handling the word of truth" (2 Timothy 2:15 NASB). There are no shortcuts to genuine exposition.[61]

Expository preaching knows no alternative for toilsome work. Yes, expository preaching is time-consuming and taxing, yet in God's eyes, this kingdom labor—among all others—merits *twofold honor*.

Personal Reflection
Having reviewed these core tenets, do you agree that they are non-negotiable for faithful expository preaching? Would you remove a tenet from the list—one that is not fundamental to pulpit ministry? Or, are these tenets intertwined and inseparable for the faithful exposition of Scripture? Moreover, if these "expository essentials" are indispensable, does your own preaching embrace all ten? If not, how might your preaching change if you did?

---

61 Mohler, *He Is Not Silent*, 66.

CHAPTER 3

Introducing the Expository Diamond

The year 2015 witnessed the unearthing of the world's second-largest diamond.[1] Its discovery brought Botswana international hype. Roughly the size of a tennis ball, the 1,111-carat stone valued at nearly $70 million.[2] However, the world's largest retrieved diamond dates back to South Africa in 1905. The behemoth Cullinan stone topped out at 3,106-carats. On account of its sheer mass, the diamond was eventually cut into nine separate stones (still a sizable family heirloom).[3]

Whether diamonds are large or small (my wife's is 1/8-carat), buyers take for granted the vast amounts of time, money, and labor required to extract them from the earth's recesses. For instance, an average of 250 tons of rock are mined per diamond.[4] Yet the annual $7 billion raw diamond industry proves the excavating, crushing, collecting, sorting,

---

1 "World's Second-Largest Diamond 'Found in Botswana,'" *BBC News*, November 19, 2015, accessed September 29, 2016, http://www.bbc.com/news/world-africa-34867929.

2 Trevor Nace, "A 1,111-Carat Diamond—The World's Second Largest—Was Found in Botswana," *Forbes News*, November 20, 2015, accessed September 29, 2016, http://www.forbes.com/sites/trevornace/2015/11/20/1111-carat-diamond-worlds-second-largest-found-botswana/#7a25622e4e50.

3 "World's Second-Largest Diamond 'Found in Botswana,'" *BBC News*, November 19, 2015, accessed September 29, 2016, http://www.bbc.com/news/world-africa-34867929.

4 "Diamond Mining- How Are Diamonds Mined and Formed?" *History TV*, March 1, 2015, accessed September 29, 2016, http://www.youtube.com/watch?v=f48PopFqzNk.

cutting, and polishing of these stones well worth the effort.[5] In fact, once cut and polished, fine diamonds gross $50 billion annually.[6]

The same cost-benefit analysis holds true for expository preaching. The psalmist declares, "The law (Torah) of Your mouth is better to me than thousands of gold and silver pieces… The sum of Your word is truth, and every one of Your righteous rules endures forever… I rejoice at Your word like one who finds great spoil" (Ps 119:72, 160, 162). Scripture in its entirety can be compared to a lavish diamond field; even though it requires extensive time, effort, and cerebral sweat to exhume its inner treasures, the weekly payout for pastors, for congregants, for guests and visitors, and ultimately for God's glory, is unrivaled. To that end, I present you with the Expository Diamond (Figure 1.1).

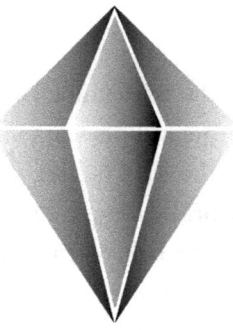

Figure 1.1. The Expository Diamond

---

[5] Ibid.
[6] Ibid.

CHAPTER 4

The Expository Diamond: Step Up

The first step in the Expository Diamond—as in any endeavor—is the most important. The entire expository process depends on and emerges from this homiletical move. Sadly, textual eagerness, busy schedules, or confidence in one's own rhetorical skillset sometimes marginalize this stepping stone. However, when a pastor *steps up,* he begins the entire expository journey in complete dependence on and submission to the Triune God. Therefore, stepping up is really about humbling oneself under—not above or on par with—God and His Word.

Naturally, then, how does a preacher step up? From the sermon's inception, he leans on the Spirit's illumination, the power of Christian prayer, and the efficacy of the text as God's written Word.

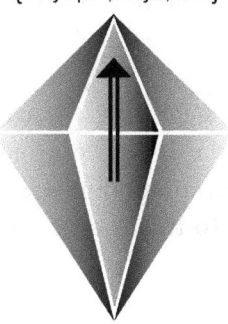

Figure 1.2. The Expository Diamond: *Step Up*

The Holy Spirit

Jesus assures His church of the Spirit's power and presence for preaching when He says, "But when *the Helper* comes, whom I will send to you from the Father, the Spirit of truth, who proceeds from the Father, He will bear witness about Me" (John 15:26; cf., John 14:16-17, 26; 16:7, 13-15). Note the difference the Holy Spirit effects in sermon preparation: (1) He illumines divine truth; and (2) He bears witness to Christ. Even Jesus received the Spirit's power before He began to publicly preach.[1] Walter Kaiser therefore reminds expositors:

> With so many instructions, steps, and cautions to be kept in mind ... exegetes are likely to throw their hands up in despair and exclaim in exasperation, "Who is sufficient for these things?" In truth, the task is enough to overwhelm almost anyone, and especially those who must gain whatever they derive from Scripture by a slow painful experience of translating, meditating, and comparing results with a number of previous commentators on the passage. That is why we must in all good conscience point to the presence and work of the Holy Spirit as the source of any confidence that we might have in our message even after we have acted most responsibly in the study and preparation of the text for proclamation.[2]

Hence, may pastors commence the homiletical journey by humbling themselves as F.R.O.G.S. (Fully Reliant on God's Spirit). He is the ultimate source for biblical guidance and interpretation. When an expositor leans on the Holy Spirit, he orients the entire sermonic process in the power, presence, and piloting of the Triune God.

Prayer

In addition, the preacher *steps up* via prayer. Paul exhorts Christians to take up the sword of the Spirit, "praying at all times in the Spirit, with all prayer and supplication" (Eph 6:18a). Preachers, do not miss Paul's ensuing petition: "To that end keep alert with all perseverance,

---

[1] See Mark 1:10-15.
[2] Walter C. Kaiser, *Toward an Exegetical Theology: Biblical Exegesis for Preaching & Teaching* (Grand Rapids: Baker Academic, 1981), 235.

making supplication for all the saints, and also for me, *that words may be given to me in opening my mouth boldly to proclaim the mystery of the gospel*, for which I am an ambassador in chains, that I may declare it boldly, as I ought to speak" (Eph 6:18b-20). Paul yokes his sermon preparation to prayer; he asks God to grant his preaching fitting words so that he can proclaim the gospel boldly. In other words, Paul steps up in prayer, and he bids the Ephesian church to join him.

So, too, Martin Luther—inspired by Psalm 119—urges three disciplines when approaching the Bible: *oratio* (prayer), *meditatio* (meditation), and *tentatio* (trial or temptation).[3] Interestingly, Luther fronts prayer for any serious rumination of Scripture. In fact, Luther advises, "You must ask that the Lord in his great mercy grant you a true understanding of his words ... for there is no one who can teach the divine words except he who is their author, as it says, 'They shall all be taught by God' (John 6:45)."[4] Luther even retorts,

> Since Holy Writ wants to be dealt with in fear and humility and penetrated more by studying with pious prayer than with keenness of intellect, therefore it is impossible for those who rely only on their intellect and rush into Scripture with dirty feet, like pigs, as those Scripture were merely human knowledge not to harm themselves and others whom they instruct.[5]

The Wittenberg Reformer knew the significance of approaching Scripture "on one's knees," and God move every expositor to begin his sermon preparation there too.

The Text

Expository preaching also necessitates that a preacher *steps up* to a text or texts of Scripture. As fundamental as this step may sound, its importance cannot be overstated. Too many sermons, though theological in nature, fail to center in a text. Granted, these sermons

---

[3] Timothy George, *Reading Scripture with the Reformers* (Downers Grove, IL: IVP Academic, 2011), 165.

[4] Ibid., quoting from *WA* 54:69. *D. Martin Luther Werke: Kritische Gesamtausgabe*, vol. 54 (Weimar: Hermann Bohlaus Nachfolger, 1883-1987), 69.

[5] Ibid., quoting from *WA* 1, 507.

might start with a text or reference one at a later point, but they seldom major in a biblical text. Can a "textually-light" homily filled with words such as grace, faith, Jesus, forgiveness, eternal life, hope, or the power of Holy Spirit be orthodox? Absolutely. However, can a "textually-light" sermon be deemed expositional? Hardly. *If God had wanted our opinion, He would have given us a topic. But God wants sermons, therefore He's given us a text!*[6] Brother, preach the text and it will pilot your theological proclamation as well.

Thus, whether preaching an assigned lectionary reading, the next passage in a book of the Bible, or tracing a theme or doctrine through Scripture, the expositor—knowing his flock—prayerfully selects a text from which to proclaim God's truth. And whichever text he chooses, his conviction stems from Jesus's words: "Heaven and earth will pass away, but My words will *never* [the strongest negation in Greek] pass away" (Luke 21:33, author's translation).[7] The expositor rests assured that Jesus continues to feed His sheep through the faithful proclamation of His Word (Heb 1:2). Furthermore, when a sermon is grounded in a text of Scripture, the homilist never has to ponder: "Did the congregation hear me today or God?"

Now that you have taken the most important step in sermon preparation—*stepping up*—you are ready for step 2.

---

6 Adapted from a preaching mentor who scolded a student for his "textually light" sermon: "If we wanted to hear what you think we would have given you a topic, but we wanted to hear what God thinks, that is why we gave you a text!" E-mail message to author, June 02, 2017.

7 Cf. Ps 18:30; 19:7; Isa 40:8; 1 Thess 2:13; 2 Tim 3:16; Heb 4:12; 1 Pet 1:25. Furthermore, "will not pass away" in Greek—*ou me* plus the future indicative—is the strongest possible way to emphatically negate something (Daniel B. Wallace, *Greek Grammar beyond the Basics* [Grand Rapids: Zondervan, 1996], 468). Hence, Jesus says there is zero chance that His words shall ever pass away. May this unswerving conviction define every Christian pulpit.

CHAPTER 5

The Expository Diamond: Step Back

Congratulations! Now that you have undertaken the first and most important step in sermon preparation, commence with step 2. This time, *step back*.

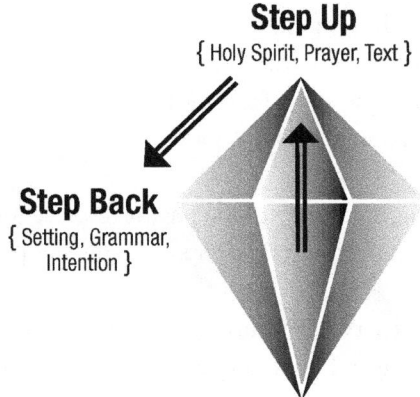

Figure 1.3. The Expository Diamond: *Step Back*

Setting

Once a preacher steps up, he continues the Expository Diamond by *stepping back* to the "then and there" of the biblical text. Intensity, labor, and cerebral sweat define this step, for it demands careful and thorough exegesis. *Exegesis* refers to the work of biblical interpretation; it literally means "to lead out" or "to draw out" from a passage what is already there.[1] So, rather than approaching a passage with the mindset: "For the most part, I already know what this text is about," the homilist does his best to approach the text "naked"—without any preconceived notions of meaning, gist, or central idea. By doing so, Scripture remains the informant, not vice versa.

The goal of exegesis is unearthing and laying bare the author's intended meaning and purpose of the text. To expose the authorial intent of a passage, the exegete studies its *sitz im leben* or original setting.[2] Haddon Robinson says, "We try to pull up our chairs to where the biblical authors sat. We attempt to work our way back into the world of the Scriptures to understand the original meaning."[3]

Or, as Bryan Chapell explains,

> Consideration of a passage's purpose ultimately forces us to ask, Why are these concerns addressed? What caused this account, these facts, or the recording of these ideas? What was the intent of the author? For what purpose did the Holy Spirit include these words in Scripture? Such questions force us to exegete the cause of a passage as well as its content.[4]

Such meticulous investigation enables the pastor to piece together the historical, cultural, and circumstantial context behind the passage and its book.

Depending on your text, two resources will help you step back: Raymond Dillard and Tremper Longman's *An Introduction to the Old*

---

[1] Walter C. Kaiser and Moises Silva, *An Introduction to Biblical Hermeneutics: The Search for Meaning* (Grand Rapids: Zondervan Publishing House, 1994), 19.

[2] *Sitz im leben* is a German phrase meaning "setting in life" or "situation in life."

[3] Haddon W. Robinson, *Biblical Preaching: The Development and Delivery of Expository Messages*, 3rd ed. (Grand Rapids: Baker Academic, 2014), 8.

[4] Bryan Chapell, *Christ-Centered Preaching: Redeeming the Expository Sermon*, 2nd ed. (Grand Rapids: Baker Academic, 2005), 49.

Testament; and D. A. Carson, Douglas J. Moo, and Leon Morris's *An Introduction to the New Testament*.[5] These works provide a backdrop for every book of the Bible, including historical background, authorship, literary analysis, structural outline, and theological message.

Grammar

Faithful exegesis requires the preacher analyze the passage's grammar as well—preferably in its original language.[6] Studying passages in Hebrew and Greek, not simply from an English translation, compares to watching a feature film or sporting event in 4K versus standard 480 definition. Both screens telecast the same picture; however, the details and clarity in 4K cannot be matched. It is worth your time (and your hearers' time) to work through the text in Hebrew or Greek.

In addition, the homilist notes these literary features as he queries the text:

- Literary Genre—First, what is the genre at the *macro* level? Is the text parable, proverb, gospel, epistle, historical narrative, poetry, song, wisdom, apocryphal, or other? Second, what is the genre at the *micro* level? Is the text exhortation, blessing, curse, warning, instruction, praise, confession, lament, or other? By noting the literary genre of passages on both levels, the expositor ensures that proper interpretive methods are used for Scripture's respective genres.[7]
- Placement—Why did the author place the passage where he did? How does your text relate to its surrounding sentences, paragraph, chapter, themed-section, book, testament, etc.? For example, why does Mark insert or "sandwich" the woman with

---

5 Raymond B. Dillard and Tremper Longman III, *An Introduction to the Old Testament*, 2nd ed. (Grand Rapids: Zondervan Publishing House, 2006); D. A. Carson, Douglas J. Moo, and Leon Morris, *An Introduction to the New Testament*, 2nd ed. (Grand Rapids: Zondervan Publishing House, 2005).

6 My exegesis has been blessed by OakTree Software's *Accordance XII* for Mac, particularly for parsing and word searches. A different software to consider for Hebrew and Greek exegesis is Faithlife's *Logos Bible Software*. Either product is worth the financial investment for your ministry.

7 To interpret literary genres in both testaments, see D. Brent Sandy and Ronald L. Giese, Jr., *Cracking Old Testament Codes: A Guide to Interpreting the Literary Genres of the Old Testament* (Nashville: B & H Academic, 1995); and Ian Paul and David Wenham, *Preaching the New Testament* (Downers Grove, IL: IVP Academic, 2013).

a discharge of blood in the middle of the scene involving Jairus' daughter (Mark 5:21ff.)?

- Vocabulary—Are certain words unique to this author, repeated, or known to carry significant theological freight? Biblical Hebrew is very picturesque. For instance, when describing God, the psalmist uses the Hebrew word *misgab* (Ps 9:9; 18:2). A *misgab* refers to a city that is not only elevated but walled—hence the English translation *stronghold*.[8] What a picture for God! The LORD is a high and impenetrable defense for all who seek refuge in Him; He is as safe as it gets for weary souls.
- Word Order—Is a particular word or phrase fronted for emphasis? In Ephesians 2:8, Paul fronts *"For by grace* you have been saved" when he could have said, "You have been saved *by grace.*" Paul's word order italicizes and underlines the source of eternal salvation: God's grace alone. Biblical Hebrew shifts word order for emphasis too. In particular, Hebrew sentence structure generally follows a verb-subject-object pattern. However, when a Hebrew writer wants to highlight the agent of the verb, he fronts the subject for a subject-verb-object order. For instance, in the Hebrew text, David fronts *"The LORD* is my shepherd" (Ps 23:1); everything else in Psalm 23 flows from this emphatic assertion: *He* makes, *He* leads, *He* restores, *You* prepare, and *You* anoint. A working knowledge of biblical Hebrew and Greek proves invaluable for noting intentional word order of texts.
- Repetition—Repetition communicates emphasis too. In the Bread of Life discourse (John 6:25-59), seven times Jesus declares that He came down (*katabainō*) from heaven. John leaves his readers with zero doubts regarding Jesus's origin and divinity. Paul employs repetition as well. In Romans 5:15-17 (ESV), "free gift" occurs five times. Combining all variants of "grace" and "gift," the Greek text exhibits seven repetitions. The exegete

---

[8] R. Laird Harris, Gleason L. Archer, Jr., and Bruce K. Waltke, eds., *A Theological Wordbook of the Old Testament*, vol. 2 (Chicago: Moody Press, 1980), 871. The two-volume set from Harris, Archer, and Waltke provides valuable insight into Hebrew vocabulary, including the theological weight of numerous words. For a deeper understanding of Greek vocabulary, see Gerhard Kittel and Gerhard Friedrich, trans., *The Theological Dictionary of the New Testament*, abridged into one volume by Geoffrey W. Bromiley (Grand Rapids: William B. Eerdmans Publishing Company, 1985).

therefore inquires, "What aspect of 'righteousness in Christ' is Paul accentuating in the text?"

- Structure—Note features such as conjunctions (coordinating and subordinating); textual interruptions, such as the sudden insertion of a proverb, song, parable, analogy, parable, or story; placement of dialogues; and the like. To take a case in point, Ephesians 1:3-14 is the second longest sentence in the Greek New Testament. Paul is so excited about God's blessings in Christ that he can barely lift his pen or pause his thought! His praise just keeps pouring out.
- Syntax—Probe the relationship between words, phrases, clauses, sentences, paragraphs, and the thematic units therein. In Greek, pay close attention to participles, prepositions, genitives, and dative cases for meaning, including variant readings in the textual apparatus. For example, Daniel Wallace contends that the preposition *pros* in Revelation 3:20 is best rendered, "I will come in *to* him" or "I will come in *toward/before* him," not "I will come *into* him."[9] Accordingly, Wallace argues that interpreting Revelation 3:20 as a salvation offering text for lost sinners violates its Greek syntax.[10]

Though toilsome at times, such literary analysis yields the governing idea or central thrust of a passage and answers the *who, what, where, when, how,* or *why* of the text.

Obviously, hermeneutics is crucial to rightly handle the Word of truth (2 Tim 2:15). A sketchy hermeneutic risks inaccurate interpretation and proclamation to God's people. Therefore, the only faithful approach to expound Holy Scripture is grammatical-historical exegesis—one which upholds the inspiration, inerrancy, historicity, and abiding relevancy of all 66 books. In addition, grammatical-historical exegesis operates on the premise that each text has one intended meaning with several

---

9 Daniel B. Wallace, *Greek Grammar Beyond the Basics: An Exegetical Syntax of the New Testament with Scripture, Subject, and Greek Word Indexes* (Grand Rapids: Zondervan, 1996), 380-82.

10 Though advanced in level, Wallace's *Greek Grammar Beyond the Basics* offers valuable assistance with Second Testament syntax. Likewise, for help with First Testament syntax, see Bruce K. Waltke and M. O'Connor, An *Introduction to Biblical Hebrew Syntax* (Winona Lake, IN: Eisenbrauns, 1990).

resultant applications. Consequently, grammatical-historical exegesis would not endorse the question: "So, what does this passage mean to you?" Rather, textual integrity asks, "What did the author mean this passage to mean?" followed by, "How does the author's intended meaning still apply to people today?"

Intention

Though technical and time-consuming, the preacher extracts the intended meaning and function of the text. The intended meaning and function answer *why* the author wrote these words and *why* he placed them in their unique context. In other words, what function were these words intended to effect among their original audience?

After a preacher *steps back*, he should be equipped to state the authorial intent or purpose of the text in one concise sentence. For example, "Moses wrote these words so that his hearers would ..." The authorial intent and purpose of Matthew 6:25-34 could be stated as follows: "Trusting in the gracious provision of the heavenly Father, that hearers would stop worrying about daily bread and prioritize the kingdom of God." Your turn. Try a familiar passage, such as Psalm 23. State its authorial intent or intended function in one precise sentence: "That the hearers would ..."[11] Specifying the authorial intent or function of a passage lays the groundwork for contemporary application and implication, which come later in the expository process.

Now that you have stepped back to the "then and there" of the text and have stated its intended meaning and function, you are ready for step 3.

---

11 "That hearers would trust the care and protection of their shepherd-God as He leads them through varied terrains in life to the celebratory feast in His eternal home," or something similar.

CHAPTER 6

The Expository Diamond: Step Out

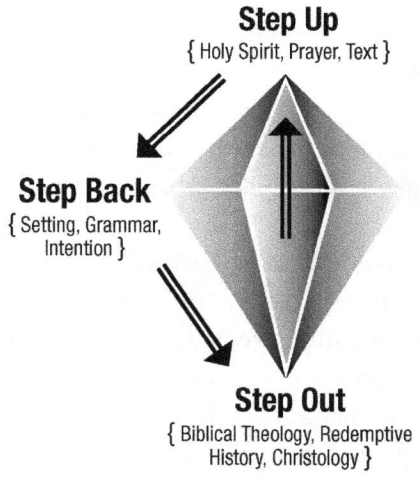

Step Up
{ Holy Spirit, Prayer, Text }

Step Back
{ Setting, Grammar, Intention }

Step Out
{ Biblical Theology, Redemptive History, Christology }

Figure 1.4. The Expository Diamond: *Step Out*

After an expositor *steps up* and *steps back*, he is ready to *step out*. Because no pericope exists on an island, the preacher determines how his text relates to the First and Second Testaments.[1] After all, the best

---

1 Because the terms *Old Testament* and *New Testament* are sometimes interpreted as dated rather than relevant in today's biblically-illiterate climate, I prefer *First Testament* and *Second Testament*. Not only does *First* and *Second Testament* communicate "connectedness" and "continuation" versus *old* and *new*, but Graeme Goldsworthy even cautions, "A continual emphasis on distinction [between the testaments] leads to separation [of the two Testaments]." Graeme Goldsworthy, *Preaching the Whole Bible as Christian Scripture: The Application of Biblical Theology to Expository Preaching* (Grand Rapids: William B. Eerdmans Publishing Company, 2000), 63.

commentary on the Bible is the Bible. Although the Bible contains sixty-six books written by forty authors over a span of nearly 1,600 years, it stands as one book by one Author with one main subject—the Messiah's first and second comings (or advents). Hence, in this step the homilist employs biblical theology, redemptive history, and Christology to interpret each passage in light of its peripheral context.

Biblical Theology

Because Scripture has one divine Author, the Holy Spirit, the entire canon remains internally self-consistent. Biblical theology examines how the parts of the Bible relate to the whole.[2] Michael Lawrence explains,

> Faithful biblical theology attempts to demonstrate what systematic theology assumes: that the Scriptures are not an eclectic, chaotic, and seemingly contradictory collection of religious writings, but rather a single story, a unified narrative that conveys a coherent and consistent message ... of the redemptive acts of God.[3]

Likewise, Graeme Goldsworthy says, "Biblical theology involves the quest for the big picture, or the overview, of biblical revelation... If we allow the Bible to tell its own story, we find a coherent and meaningful whole ... which tells the story of creation and the saving plan of God."[4]

Once an expositor specifies the author's intended meaning and function of the text, he applies biblical theology to survey the passage in its larger context: paragraph, chapter, unit, book, testament, and canon. Look for themes in your text that track longitudinally through both Testaments—themes such as creation, light, seed, mountain, sacrifice, priesthood, tabernacle, temple, water, cloud, king, or new creation. Once again, Lawrence advises,

> Using the tools of biblical theology, we then consider the point of the text in light of where the text falls in redemptive-history. In

---

2 Goldsworthy, *Preaching the Whole Bible*, 64.

3 Michael Lawrence, *Biblical Theology in the Life of the Church: A Guide for Ministry* (Wheaton, IL: Crossway, 2010), 26, 38.

4 Goldsworthy, *Preaching the Whole Bible*, 22.

what epoch of God's saving work does it occur? Is there something new or distinct going on from what has happened before [in Scripture]? Has a promise been fulfilled at one level? Has a type been developed or more clearly defined? Then ... we ask ourselves, what's the point of the text in light of the whole canon—that is to say, in light of Christ's work on the cross and his promised return? Do we see a final fulfillment of a promise or a type? Is discontinuity introduced that marks a change, development or expansion of a previous promise? In what way is continuity maintained? ... The result is that we are now able to teach or preach on our text, not as if it's a pearl on a string, unrelated to the rest of Scripture, but as it really is, one section of an entire tapestry that is inextricably and organically connected to the whole.[5]

From this enlarged vantage point of Scripture, preachers stand prepared to make individual and corporate application from the text.

For instance, the following passages link thematically with Psalm 23 and its "Shepherd-God" theme: Genesis 48:15; Psalm 28:9; Psalm 80:1; Isaiah 40:11; Ezekiel 34; Micah 5-7; John 10; 1 Peter 2; and Revelation 7:17. The First Testament foreshadows just how far God's personal and provisional care would extend for His flock. The Second Testament proclaims the Shepherd-God who became flesh; laid down His life for the sheep; took it up again on the third day; gathers lost sheep into His fold; and tends them to all eternity.

Suggested books to enrich your understanding of biblical theology include G. K. Beale's *A New Testament Biblical Theology*; Graeme Goldsworthy's *The Transformation of the Old Testament in the New*; and Thomas R. Schreiner's *The King in His Beauty*.[6]

Redemptive History

Goldsworthy explains that redemptive history or "salvation history" in exposition "recognizes a specific history as the framework within

---

5 Lawrence, *Biblical Theology in the Life of the Church*, 181.

6 G. K. Beale, *A New Testament Biblical Theology: The Transformation of the Old Testament in the New* (Grand Rapids: Baker, 2011); Graeme Goldsworthy, *According to Plan: The Unfolding Revelation of God in the Bible* (Downers Grove, IL: InterVarsity, 2002); and Thomas R. Schreiner, *The King in His Beauty: A Biblical Theology of the Old and New Testaments* (Grand Rapids: Baker, 2013).

which God has worked, is now working, and will work in the future."[7] Goldsworthy continues to write that redemptive history "implies a recognition that Yahweh, the God of Israel, and the God and Father of our Lord Jesus Christ, is the Lord of history"; He alone is reigning over time and events to redeem "a great multitude ... from every nation, from all tribes and peoples and languages (Rev 7:9)."[8] Likewise, Sydney Greidanus says,

> The Old Testament proclaims God's mighty acts of redemption. These acts reach a climax in the New Testament when God sends his Son. Redemptive history is the mighty river that runs from the old covenant to the new and holds the two together... There is a progression in redemptive history, but it is one redemptive history... In other words, a single, God-guided, redemptive history is the basis, the foundation, or the unity of the Old and New Testaments.[9]

Greidanus adds, "Accordingly, the way of redemptive-historical progression sees every Old Testament text and its addressees in the context of God's dynamic history, which progresses steadily and reaches its climax in the life, death, and resurrection of Jesus Christ and ultimately in the new creation."[10]

To further assist expositors with a redemptive-historical understanding of their text, Daniel Doriani offers the following guidance:

> Redemptive-historical preaching (RHP) emphasizes the unity of the history of redemption and the centrality of Christ in that history. It places every passage of Scripture in its historical context and asks questions such as: Where are this event and text located in the history of redemption? What are the traits of the covenant that govern the era? What do the people know about God's

---

7 Goldsworthy, *Preaching the Whole Bible*, 27, 88.
8 Goldsworthy, *Preaching the Whole Bible*, 28.
9 Sydney Greidanus, *Preaching Christ from the Old Testament: A Contemporary Hermeneutical Method* (Grand Rapids: William B. Eerdmans Publishing Company, 1999), 48.
10 Ibid., 237.

character, redemption, and ethic? How does this text add to that knowledge? RHP emphasizes the progressive, organic revelation of God's truth, disclosed ever more fully in successive covenants with Adam, Noah, Abraham, Moses, David, and Jesus, in whose death and resurrection biblical history reaches its climax... RHP traces the unfolding of the plan of salvation, seeking hints of the Christ, though he may not be mentioned by name, in all Scripture, so as to proclaim him from all Scripture (Luke 24).[11]

Doriani reiterates,

Indeed, the Bible is one long drama that begins when God creates heaven and earth, and ends when he restores them. The intervening chapters describe God's achievement of his aims, not humans reaching out to God. Redemptive-historical preaching exalts the God who saves with infinite mercy. It opposes moralizing application, denouncing narrative expositions that focus on human participants as exemplars of good or bad behavior. It cannot tolerate sermons (and hymns) that fail to name and honor Christ, that propound general moral or spiritual instruction that any theist could find agreeable. It safeguards an essential of interpretation: it keeps the broad context of every Scripture firmly in view.[12]

Therefore, when *stepping out* from a text, Greidanus says that "Christian preachers need only locate their preaching-text in the sweep of redemptive history to sense its movement to Christ."[13]

To take a case in point, let's apply redemptive history to the Tower of Babel episode (Gen 11:1-9). The narrative ends with mass confusion and continental divide. Therefore, the question looms: What will become of God's promise to provide mankind with a redemptive Seed (Gen 3:15)? After all, humanity is dazed, confused, and oceans apart. Two biblical truths come to mind. First, the reign of God is neither shocked nor confounded by world events; He is Lord of all. Because

---

11 Daniel M. Doriani, *Putting the Truth to Work: The Theory and Practice of Biblical Application* (Phillipsburg, NJ: P & R Publishing, 2001), 294.
12 Doriani, *Putting the Truth to Work*, 296.
13 Greidanus, *Preaching Christ from the Old Testament*, 237-238.

God's sovereignty has no bounds, His redemptive plan continues to unfold and progress in, through, and in spite of man's sin. Second, by God's predetermination, He has already elected one individual from the scattered masses through whom Messiah will still come: Abram. It is in Messiah—Abram's (and Eve's) ultimate Seed (*zera'*)—that perfect oneness and unity will once again be possible and effected among the dispersed nations, but only in Messiah and the outpouring of His Spirit (i.e., see Acts 2:6-11, 22-24; Gal 3:26-29; Rev 7:9-10).[14]

Christology

Indeed, biblical theology and redemptive history culminate in Jesus Christ; He is the focal point and goal of all biblical exposition.[15] This understanding of Scripture is known as the Christological Principle, or "the principle that all Scripture is Christocentric, centered on the person and work of Christ."[16] Timothy Keller says, "To show how a text fits into its whole canonical context, then, is to show how it points to Christ and the gospel salvation, the big idea of the whole Bible."[17] Moreover, Bryan Chapell explains,

> The necessity of grace in balanced preaching inevitably points both preacher and parishioner to the work of Christ as the only proper center of a sermon. Christ-centered preaching is not merely evangelistic, nor is it confined to a few gospel accounts. It perceives the whole of Scripture as revelatory of God's redemptive plan and sees every passage within this context—a pattern Jesus himself introduced (Luke 24:27) ... Thus, no aspect of revelation can be thoroughly understood or explained in isolation from some aspect

---

14 For additional insight on redemptive history, I highly recommend Graeme Goldsworthy, *Preaching the Whole Bible as Christian Scripture: The Application of Biblical Theology to Expository Preaching* (Grand Rapids: William B. Eerdmans Publishing Company, 2000); and Sidney Greidanus, *Preaching Christ from the Old Testament: A Contemporary Hermeneutical Method* (Grand Rapids: William B. Eerdmans Publishing Company, 1999).

15 See 1 Cor 1:23; 2:2.

16 James W. Voelz, *What Does This Mean? Principles of Biblical Interpretation in the Post-Modern World* (St. Louis: CPH, 1997), 362.

17 Timothy Keller, *Preaching: Communicating Faith in an Age of Skepticism* (New York: Viking, 2015), 48.

of Christ's redeeming work.[18]

In light of Scripture's Christocentricity, Graeme Goldsworthy implores expositors:

> To the evangelical preacher, then, I would address one simple but pointed question, a question every one of us should ask ourselves as we prepare to preach… How does this passage of Scripture, and consequently my sermon, testify to Christ? There are two main grounds for this question. The first … is that Jesus claims to be the subject of all Scripture. The second is the overall structure of biblical revelation, which finds its coherence only in the person and work of Christ… Given these considerations of the nature of the Bible, I can think of no more challenging question for preacher's self-evaluation than to ask whether the sermon was a faithful exposition of the way the text testifies to Christ.[19]

When an expositor *steps out*, he is equipped (and eager) to preach Christ from any portion of Scripture, thereby affirming the cohesiveness of both Testaments in their witness to Christ.[20]

In Scripture's Christocentricity, some texts focus more on the cross of Christ (humiliation), while other texts focus more on the crown of Christ (exaltation). Texts that point to the cross emphasize the suffering, substitutionary, and savior motifs of Messiah, whereas texts that point to His crown accentuate the risen, reigning, and returning King. Hence, when preparing to preach Christ from your text, discern if the text contains cross or crown ornamentation, but do not keep your text from reaching its climax in the person, work, and teachings of Jesus Christ.

One final point to consider: if an expositor is going to err in Christ-centered interpretation and proclamation, err on the side of preaching too much Christ rather than too little Christ. Granted, Christocentric-preaching does not give homilists license to venture into allegory or other speculative or fanciful connections *in* or *between* texts; however,

---

18 Chapell, *Christ-Centered Preaching*, 40, 276.
19 Goldsworthy, *Preaching the Whole Bible*, 21.
20 Vaughan Roberts, *God's Big Picture: Tracing the Storyline of the Bible* (Downers Grove, IL: IVP Books, 2002), 163.

the preacher looks for Jesus where Jesus says He can be found (see John 5:39, 46; Luke 24:25-27; 44-47).[21]

Now that your sermon preparation has *stepped up*, *stepped back*, and *stepped out*, you are ready for the final facet of the Expository Diamond.

---

21 Keller, *Preaching: Communicating Faith in an Age of Skepticism* is an inspiring read for preaching Christ from all Scripture.

CHAPTER 7

The Expository Diamond: Step Forward

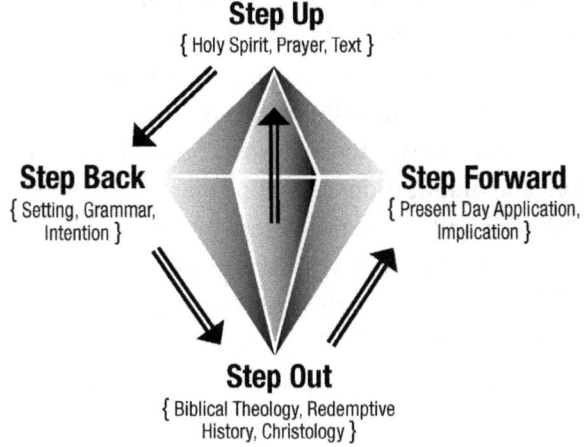

Figure 1.5. The Expository Diamond: *Step Forward*

If my goal was symmetry, then *Step Forward* would read *explanation*, *application*, and *implication*. After all, expository preaching explains or unfolds the meaning of a text to its hearers, especially after receiving Spirit-illumined insight from stepping up, stepping back, and stepping out. I assume, however, that preachers will naturally explain the intended meaning of texts *then* and *now* as they steer toward—or weave in and out of—Spirit-empowered application and implication in the lives of hearers today.

Jesus exemplifies application and implication in preaching when He concludes the Sermon on the Mount:

> Everyone then who hears these words of mine and does them will be like a wise man who built his house on the rock. And the rain fell, and the floods came, and the winds blew and beat on that house, but it did not fall, because it had been founded on the rock. And everyone who hears these words of mine and does not do them will be like a foolish man who built his house on the sand. And the rain fell, and the floods came, and the winds blew and beat against that house, and it fell, and great was the fall of it. (Matt 7:24-27)

Jesus closes His sermon with both application (so what?) and implication (now what?). He summons His hearers to not just hear His teachings, but to go forth in faith and live them.[1] Indeed, Jesus declares that every disciple who hears His words *and* does them is prepared for this life and for the Consummation, yet individuals who hear Jesus's words and disregard them will crumble in judgment.[2]

Peter and Paul drive their gospel proclamation toward hearer application and implication as well. Peter declares in his Pentecost sermon, "Repent and be baptized every one of you in the name of Jesus Christ for the forgiveness of your sins, and you will receive the gift of the Holy Spirit. For the promise is for you and for your children and for all who are far off, everyone whom the Lord our God calls to Himself" (Acts 2:38-39). Moreover, Paul proclaims in his Mars Hill sermon,

> Being then God's offspring, we ought not to think that the divine being is like gold or silver or stone, an image formed by the art and imagination of man. The times of ignorance God overlooked, but now he commands all people everywhere to repent, because he has fixed a day on which he will judge the world in righteousness by a man whom he has appointed; and of this he has given assurance to all by raising him from the dead. (Acts 17:29-31)

The Holy Spirit works through both appeals. Three thousand souls

---

[1] In James 1:22-27, Jesus's half-brother reiterates the importance of being both hearers and doers of God's Word.

[2] See Luke 3:1-14 for a fine example of application and implication in John the Baptist's proclamation too.

receive Peter's word and are baptized on Pentecost, and a handful of listeners believe the gospel Paul proclaims and join him, including Dionysius (the Areopagite), Damaris, and others who are with them (see Acts 2:41; 17:32-34).

Can twenty-first century homilists expect similar kingdom results when they faithfully expound Scripture? Absolutely! When and where God's Word is faithfully preached, three things happen. Some unbelievers, led by the Holy Spirit, hear the gospel and respond in repentance and faith (Acts 2:41). Current Christians hear the Word and have their faith built up, strengthened, and affirmed (Acts 16:5; 20:2). Sadly, other non-Christians hear the same Word but continue in hardness of heart and unbelief as they reject the Holy Spirit's work (Acts 17:32-34; 26:28). One fact, though, remains certain: the faithful exposition of God's Word is never neutral. The LORD Himself attests, "For as the rain and the snow come down from heaven and do not return there but water the earth, making it bring forth and sprout, giving seed to the sower and bread to the eater, so shall my word be that goes out from my mouth; it shall not return to me empty, but it shall accomplish that which I purpose, and shall succeed in the thing for which I sent it" (Isa 55:10-11). Therefore, fellow expositors, trust the sufficiency and efficacy of God's Word. God will accomplish His eternal purposes through His preached Word. Faithful exposition is never done in vain.

Because application and implication are indispensable to expository preaching, this step of the Expository Diamond merits additional attention. Bryan Chapell accentuates,

> Application—at least its general direction—must precede final decisions about structure, exegetical emphases, wording, and even the tone of a message, or else the preacher will be designing a highway without knowing its destination... Application gives ultimate meaning to exposition... This means that until a preacher provides application, exposition remains incomplete.[3]

In other words, application and implication fasten parachutes to

---

3 Bryan Chapell, *Christ-Centered Preaching: Redeeming the Expository Sermon*, 2nd ed. (Grand Rapids: Baker Academic, 2005), 213.

exposition; they impart textual relevance to the gathered. Gospel-powered application and implication effect change in hearers' lives. The Holy Spirit works through their proclamation to reshape hearers' attitudes, choices, motives, thoughts, beliefs, behaviors, works, and words (2 Cor 3:17-18).

However, when preachers neglect application (so what?) and implication (now what?), congregants are left to piece-meal meaning and application for themselves—if at all. Such homiletical negligence breeds fertile soil for the heinous assumption that Scripture has no real meaning for present-day life. Accordingly, Ramesh Richard admonishes pastors, "We cannot take it for granted that they [the hearers] have understood the application. Application is not automatic. Actually, people are not prone to apply truths to themselves. They would rather apply them to someone else!"[4]

What steps can preachers take to ensure rightful application and implication in every sermon? First, be mindful of different cross-sections within your audience—including youth, students, singles, dating singles, married, newly married, married with children, married without children, single parents, divorced, elderly, empty nesters, widows, widowers, blue collar, white collar, graduates, unemployed, retirees, special needs, and those receiving clinical treatment, etc. Consider how the intention of your text applies to various demographics in the congregation. For instance, when preaching on *worry* from Matthew 6:25-34, I Googled the top five things teenagers worry about, plus the top five things parents of teenagers worry about. This simple search helped me speak relevantly to two specific segments within the congregation. Granted, preachers cannot cover each sector of the congregation every Sunday, but population awareness keeps textual application specific and varied from week to week.

Second, know your flock. For pastors to really know their people, they must spend time among their sheep. Observe. Listen. Converse. Care. Inquire. No other way exists. John Stott counsels under-shepherds:

> The best preachers ... know the people of their district and congregation and understand the human scene with its pain and

---

[4] Ramesh Richard, *Preparing Expository Sermons: A Seven-Step Method for Biblical Preaching* (Grand Rapids: Baker Books, 2001), 49.

pleasure. Shut your mouth and open your eyes and ears to the community. Ask people questions and get them talking. Have them tell us about their home and family, job, expertise, spare-time interests, what makes you tick? How your Christian faith motivates you? Which problems do they have that impede their believing or inhibit them from applying their faith to their life?[5]

The more a preacher loves and understands his congregation—including his professional and volunteer staff—the more concrete and personal he can speak God's Word into their lives. After all, does any preacher want the alpha wolf (Satan) and his demonic hounds (Matt 7:15) spending more time with the sheep than Christ's under-shepherd does? Hence, grab (or open) your weekly calendar and block out time to be with your people. Yes, clergy are busy, but this fundamental investment yields high homiletical returns.

Third, envision what the fullness of the text's intention would look like among your worshipers—including yourself. When Jesus warns His disciples about materialism in Luke 12, He says, "Sell your possessions, and give to the needy. Provide yourselves with money bags that do not grow old, with a treasure in the heavens that does not fail, where no thief approaches and no moth destroys" (v. 33). What would the fullness of Jesus's words look like in the church? Acts 2 paints a beautiful picture:

> So those who received his [Peter's] word were baptized, and there were added that day about three thousand souls. And they devoted themselves to the apostles' teaching and the fellowship, to the breaking of bread and the prayers... And all who believed were together and had all things in common. And they were *selling their possessions and belongings and distributing the proceeds to all*, as any had need. (vv. 41-45)

The Holy Spirit empowers the newly baptized to act on Jesus's words and aid fellow believers in meager times. In response to Jesus's words in Luke 12, the Spirit put it on the hearts of my first congregation to have a "possessions sale." We challenged every member and attender

---

[5] John R. W. Stott, *Between Two Worlds: The Challenge of Preaching Today* (Grand Rapids: William B. Eerdmans Publishing Company, 1982), 192.

to sell at least one possession that hurt to part with—not leftover junk that has been collecting dust in an attic, closet, or garage. The Spirit moved people to sell collectibles, computers, even a Fender guitar. The result: the congregation raised enough funds to dig two freshwater wells in Africa. God be praised for effecting obedience to Jesus's words and for many people being blessed by their sacrificial love. The joy and excitement were contagious to say the least. Moreover, Jesus did not just commission His church that "it is more blessed to give than to receive," but He embodied it Himself (Acts 20:35).

Fourth, as you work through the implication of the text, ask what gospel-driven, Spirit-empowered change God wants to effect in your hearers. Does God—through the preached text—summon His people to trust, hope, repent, believe, pray, abstain, give, rejoice, praise, surrender, submit, or other? For instance, if you were preaching on 1 Corinthians 6:12-20, what might the application (so what?) and the implication (now what?) of the text entail? The "so what" of the text could preach as follows: "Our lives are not our own to live as we please. We are under new ownership. We have been bought at an exceedingly high price—the life-blood of Jesus Christ, and His Spirit has made His abode in us. Therefore, we are holy ground, living temples of the Holy Spirit." Paul's words proclaim beautiful gospel. In addition, the "now what" of the text could exhort hearers in this way:

> Because of our new ownership, what would be inappropriate to say, think, or do in church (i.e., show a XXX film or have exotic dancers) is even more inappropriate and entirely out of place in us—God's true temple! Therefore, in the power of the Holy Spirit, let us flee all sexual immorality and glorify the God *in us* with lives of purity and chaste obedience. What would sexual purity look like among us, myself included? If you're wrestling with pornography, repent and join a support group; you cannot do it alone, nor do you have to. If you're living with your fiancé before marriage, repent and live separately until your special day. If you're involved with another person, repent, sever the relationship, and come clean today. If your mind replays lustful fantasies, repent, and in the vigor of the Holy Spirit, take those thoughts captive to the highest power—the Lord Jesus Christ (2 Cor 10:5). My friends, as

we work by grace to live lives of sexual purity, we reflect Christ in this stained world and we give witness to the fact that God is in His holy temple (pointing to my heart). By His might and for His glory. Amen.

Gospel-motivated application always gives rise to Spirit-empowered implication in the lives of hearers today.

To summarize, preachers must work the entire Expository Diamond with every text:

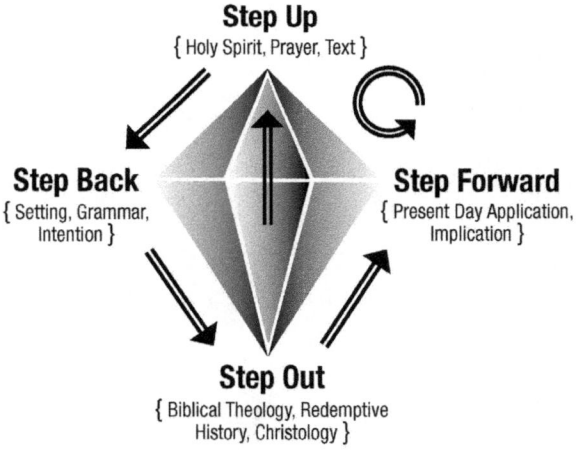

Figure 1.6. The Full Expository Diamond

As preachers step up, step back, step out, and step forward, not only can they be assured that their exposition is faithful to the intention of text, but they can also trust that the gathered will hear God speaking relevantly into their lives. When homilists expound Scripture for *all* its worth, God is glorified and His kingdom comes.

CHAPTER 8

The Expository Diamond: Expository Pitfalls

Faithful exposition necessitates a word of caution. As a homilist works the Expository Diamond on a weekly basis, he must persistently guard against three expository pitfalls. Irrespective of reasoning or circumstances, these pitfalls result when the preacher bypasses one or more steps of the Expository Diamond.

The Tip-Toe
The first pitfall occurs when a homilist skips directly from the first step (Step Up) to the fourth step (Step Forward).

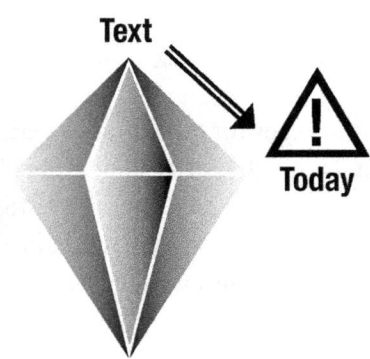

Figure 1.7. Expository Pitfalls: *The Tip-Toe*

Whether his reasoning is busyness or laziness, the result remains the same: shallow, surface-level preaching. Michael Green comments, "This is the age of the sermonette, and sermonettes make Christianettes."[1] It follows, then, that the first pitfall is rightly termed *The Tip-Toe*. The preacher merely prances across the topsoil of Scripture, snubbing a passage's historical, cultural, grammatical, contextual, canonical, and Christological sub-terrain. Unfortunately, story-upon-story often characterizes the depth and flow of *Tip-Toe* preaching.

Misinterpretation

The second expository pitfall plummets a sermon toward *misinterpretation*. Misinterpretation happens when the preacher bypasses the second step (Step Back) of the Expository Diamond and carts a text immediately to Christ.

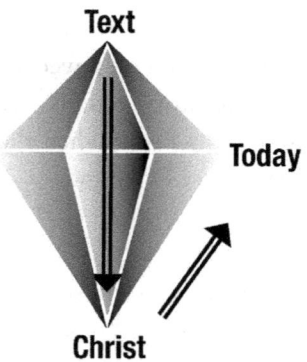

Figure 1.8. Expository Pitfalls: *Misinterpretation*

Once again, the expositor dismisses the pericope's original setting and authorial intent. Granted, Jesus distinguishes Himself as *the* hermeneutic of Scripture (cf. Luke 24:27, 44; John 5:39, 46), yet to disavow how the Holy Spirit intended a passage to function among its first recipients leaves a homilist open to misinterpret, misuse, mishandle, and misapply the text today, even with its Christology.

---

1 Dan Dumas, ed., *A Guide to Expository Ministry: Guide Book No. 003* (Louisville: SBTS Press, 2012), 18.

Legalism

The third expository pitfall is *legalism*. Legalism occurs every time a pastor misses the third step (Step Out) of the Expository Diamond.

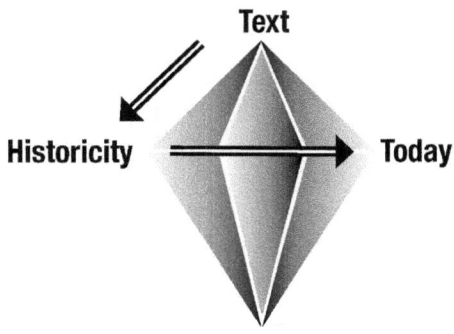

Figure 1.9. Expository Pitfalls: *Legalism*

Because no Scripture in its immediate or peripheral context can be severed from the person and work of Jesus Christ, jumping from a text's historicity and intention to contemporary application and implication without Messianic fulfillment merely imposes the burdens and demands of the Law upon its hearers. Without the perfect obedience and sacrifice of Jesus that was promised in the First Testament and realized in the Second Testament, audiences are left with "emulate Moses," "defeat your Goliaths," "work harder on the Ten Commandments," and "be Good Samaritans." A homily without Jesus might suit a mosque, synagogue, temple, or interfaith service on Capitol Hill, but under no circumstance should a Christ-less sermon be found in His church on earth. "For by works of the law no human being will be justified in His sight, since through the law comes knowledge of sin. But now the righteousness of God has been manifested apart from the law, although the Law and the Prophets bear witness to it—the righteousness of God through faith in Jesus Christ for all who believe" (Rom 3:20-22). Without Jesus there can be no faithful exposition of God's Word: period!

CHAPTER 9

Pull It Together: Destination Preaching and Sermon Structure

Have you heard of *backward design*? Other terms include *backward planning* or *backward mapping*. First introduced by Jay McTighe and Grant Wiggins in 1998, backward design

> begins with the objectives of a unit or course—what students are expected to learn and be able to do—and then proceeds "backward" to create lessons that achieve those desired goals… The basic rationale motivating backward design is that starting with the end goal, rather than a starting with the first lesson chronologically delivered during a unit or course, helps teachers design a sequence of lessons, problems, projects, presentations, assignments and <u>assessments</u> that result in students achieving the academic goals of a course or unit—that is, actually learning what they were expected to learn.[1]

Backward design readily applies to sermon preparation too. When you work the Expository Diamond and state the intended function of

---

1 Grant Wiggins and Jay McTighe, *Understanding by Design*, 2nd ed. (Alexandria, VA: Association for Supervision and Curriculum Development, 2005), quoted in "The Glossary of Education Reform," last updated December 13, 2013, accessed May 20, 2017, http://edglossary.org/backward-design.

the text in one sentence (i.e., "That the hearers would ..."), the function statement establishes the end point or goal of your sermon. In other words, the function statement paints the target or desired outcome the author intended (i.e., authorial intent) the text to effect in its hearers. Hence, start your sermon outline there—at the "end point" or "textual goal"; next, sequence your homily to move hearers toward that biblical destination.

In fact, think of your sermon as if you are a commercial airline pilot. You are about to take many souls with you to a desired destination. The pilot, however, does not commence with his current location; rather, he or she begins with the final destination in mind. Once that airport has been established, the pilot charts the best flight path to get there. In the same way, the intended function of a text generates the final destination or goal of the sermon; hence, the preacher sets the homiletical heading to that biblical location or textual end.

Furthermore, once an aircraft is boarded and ready for departure, every flight faces three critical moments for success: (1) the takeoff; (2) the flight; and (3) the landing. Let's talk about these pivotal moments in your preaching.

The Takeoff

A naval veteran once told me that the hardest part for any flight occurs in that moment when the nose of the aircraft abandons the runway (officially termed *rotation*). At that point, the force of gravity and mass of the aircraft bear down on the rear wheels of the plane. What happens in that moment determines whether "the bird" will generate enough lift to go airborne. If the aircraft leaves the ground, however, it gains altitude by the second, and the sky is the limit.

Consequently, the introduction of a sermon is crucial to the success of the entire flight (homily). The preacher must make sure that the sermon generates enough lift—stimulates enough attention, curiosity, and interest—to leave the ground with everyone on board. To accomplish this task, a sermon's introduction needs to do three things. First, an introduction needs to capture the audience's attention. Yes, worshipers are gathered, but preachers cannot assume that they are "locked in the upright position" and ready to listen. As clergy, we do not know what kind of week our people have had or what afternoon plans they might be pondering. Thus, we need to grab their attention and do so quickly, lest we give their minds permission to wander. What is the most effective method for preachers to seize hearers' attention? Options abound, including appropriate humor, a statistic, verse or refrain from a song, quote, story, probing question, poem, movie segment, video clip, Facebook post, period of silence, even prayer ... something that communicates that the preacher has a word worth listening to.

Second, once the homilist earns the people's attention, the introduction needs to present the sermon's theme. This homiletical move ensures that "attention grabbers" are not simply for fun's sake, but they actually link to the day's text. The shift can be as simple as, "today, God wants to talk to us about ..." which cues hearers into the destination and establishes relevancy.

Finally, the introduction needs to transition the hearers into the text itself. Preachers can point listeners to the first verse or verses on a screen, bulletin cover, fill-in-the-blank sermon notes, or perhaps have everyone read the text together. Either way, God's Word pilots the sermon; He is the One conversing with the people.

The following is an introduction from a sermon on worry (Luke 12:22-31):

> A man was spotted running down the surgical wing of a hospital. A nurse stopped him and asked: "Sir, what's going on? Is everything okay?" Panting, the man answered, "I heard the nurse say: "Don't worry. It's a simple procedure. I'm sure everything will go just fine." "Oh," said the nurse who'd stopped him, "she was just trying to comfort you before the operation." "You don't understand," the man replied, "the nurse wasn't talking to me; she was talking to the surgeon!" (pause for the laughing to subside)
>
> Today we're going to talk about something that's as common as currency, even in church: worry. Right? Sometimes we worry about big things. "Who will our children marry? Will we be able to retire at a decent age? Will chemo and radiation work?" Sometimes we worry about small things. "Traffic is heavy; am I going to be late? What should I wear tomorrow? What if my paper comes back with a "C"?" Other times we worry about silly things. "Did I start

the right player in fantasy football this week? What if there's an earthquake while I'm stopped under this overpass?"

Yet when we look at Jesus's words in Luke 12, He has a different path for us than worry. In fact, Jesus has a way that we can win over worry. Let's take a look at the top of your sermon notes. Luke records ...

Speaking a brief prayer between the introduction and the body of a sermon can also create a powerful transition into the text, especially a petition asking God for pliable hearts that fully ingest His Word.

The Flight
Once a sermon lifts off with everyone on board, the longest leg of the flight begins—cruising altitude, or the body of the sermon. In my experience with commercial airlines, two kinds of flights exist: direct flights (officially *non-stop flights*) and connecting flights (officially *multiple-leg flights*). The same basic structures apply to preaching.

Direct Flights
Sometimes a text lends itself to a direct-flight sermon structure, one that continuously unfolds the progression of the text or retells its story in detail. Direct-flight sermon structures work well with biblical narrative and parables. For example, when I preached on Genesis 29:31-30:24 and the fertility marathon between Leah and Rachel (note how Jacob quietly enjoys the ride ... pun intended), I simply retold the narrative with its dirty details (children were dismissed from the sanctuary for this particular sermon). As we neared the final destination of the sermon, I stressed God's covenant faithfulness—even in the filth of human sin. As Jacob rotates between four different women, God still works to fulfill His promises to Abraham.[2] For final application and implication, I ran Abraham's d-y-S-f-u-n-c-t-*I*-o-*N*-a-l family tree (note the real root word of dySfunctIoN) all the way to Jesus. According to Galatians 3:27-29, Abraham's promises and family tree are ours via baptism into Christ. What a gift! What a clean-up act of grace for *all* of God's children!

---

[2] This sermon was inspired by Dale Ralph Davis, *The Word Became Fresh: How to Preach from Old Testament Narrative Texts* (Fearn, Scotland: Mentor, 2012), 39-42.

Moreover, this narrative simply did not fit a point one, point two, point three, or point four sermon structure.

Direct flights can also take the form of an inductive investigation. Inductive homilies raise a significant question at the beginning of the sermon. The rest of the sermon journeys through a biblical text and leads hearers toward resolution, or the answer, along with final application and implication. For instance, an inductive approach would suit Psalm 139. The introduction could sound like the following:

> What does it mean that God is your Creator? Have you thought about that? What does it mean that God created you? That's an enormous question, and one that the church has been confessing in its creeds for more than 1,500 years. Yet, what does it really mean for you to profess that God is your Creator? The psalmist unpacks that question for us in Psalm 139, as well as what it means for us in relation to God and to other people. Let's take a look.

Connecting Flights

The second kind of flight plan makes connections or stops at specific points in route to the destination. This sermon structure is deductive by nature; it expounds main points and sub-points of the text. Deductive sermons state the intended meaning of the text in the introduction; then point-by-point, the sermon works through the progression of the text to show how the deduction was reached.

Though time consuming, diagramming a text exposes the author's argument and helps the expositor create a point-by-point homiletical outline. Generally, indicative verbs and imperative verbs generate the main points of a sermon outline, while subordinating conjunctions and dependent clauses form sub-points that answer the who, what, where, when, how, or why of the main clauses. Pauline epistles often lend themselves to multi-point homilies. Below is a sermon outline of Philippians 4:10-20:

"The Beauty of Gospel Partnership"
I. Gospel partnership occasions great joy in the Lord (v. 10).
II. Gospel partnership manifests a deep-seated and mutual concern for others regardless of circumstance or need

(vv. 11-13).
III. Gospel partnership willingly shares in another's hardships, including financial sacrifice (vv. 14-16).
    a. It's not about the gifts themselves that support gospel ministry, but what such gifts signify.
    b. Such gospel support incurs eschatological interest and emits a fragrant aroma to God.
IV. Gospel partnership is fully convinced of God's gracious provision in Christ Jesus (v. 19).
V. Gospel partnership is all for God's glory (v. 20).

Thomas Schreiner's *Interpreting the Pauline Epistles* proves helpful for tracking Pauline arguments and outlining texts for multiple-leg sermons.[3]

How does a preacher know which sermon structure to use? Do not approach a text with a preconceived structure in mind. Instead, work the Expository Diamond and allow the text to determine which homiletical path best communicates its intention to your hearers. Whichever flight path you choose—direct or connecting—it is imperative that the structure be textual. In flight lingo, do not pull a "touch and go" with the text; rather, work the text for the duration of the flight.

Furthermore, as with flying, continuous sermon structures and multiple-leg sermon structures need to convey a sense of progress. Hearers should feel themselves moving toward a final destination. To that end, with "connecting flights" I construct a ½-page, fill-in-the-blank sermon sheet for worshippers to fill out as we unfold the points and sub-points of the text. Not only do sermon notes enhance hearer attention and retention, but they also give hearers a way to track the progress of the flight.

The Landing

The Law of Gravity states, "What goes up must come down." As the homily nears the intended and final destination of the text, the preacher prepares to stick the landing. After all, congregants have been known

---

3 Thomas R. Schreiner, *Interpreting the Pauline Epistles* (Grand Rapids: Baker Book House, 1990).

to remind their pastors that worshipers, like airplanes, can only carry so much fuel (i.e., pay attention for so long). Hence, there comes a time when the pilot must land the aircraft. Likewise, the preacher wants the sermon to make a successful "touch down," one that leaves the gospel resounding in hearts and minds and empowers life transformation. In the absence of a well-planned and intentional landing, hearers are left dangling, having to piece together their own "take home" from the message.

As a result, conclusions, like introductions, need to do three things. First, most of the time, but not always, conclusions cue hearers into the final approach. For instance, when pilots first slow the engines and dip the nose of the aircraft, passengers know the initial approach or descent has begun. The final destination draws nigh. In the same way, conclusions communicate, "Hey! We are almost there! This is the moment we have been building toward. Make sure your seats are upright and at full attention." The tone of the pastor's voice; the pace of his words; his posture in the pulpit or up front; his poise; and his demeanor should convey to hearers: "We are bringing this sermon in for a landing."

Second, conclusions encapsulate final exhortation; they bring the homily to its desired destination: the gospel-motivated, Spirit-empowered implication and intention of the text. This segment of the conclusion is the opportune time for the preacher's most powerful story, illustration, quote, video clip, or living example from the faith community. Leverage the final exhortation to make the intended function of the text resound for the gathered.

Third, after final exhortation, conclude the sermon in a timely manner. In other words, pull up to the concourse and "let God's people go." Remember, no one enjoys a false landing (officially *a go-around*). How many of you have sat through a sermon with two, three, or even four false landings? Do you remember your frustration as a hearer? Maybe not if you were the preacher! Thus, give the final *Amen*. Speak Paul's blessing in Philippians 4:7 over the people. Set a hook for next week's sermon, or close with a summative prayer. Either way, it is time to sit down and continue with the next part of the worship service.

To illustrate, here is a conclusion I crafted for an Easter sermon on Romans 8:11. The sermon focused on the "The Unstoppable Power of Easter." The fourth and final point of my outline asserted, "Death is but a prelude, for the grand display of Easter-power is yet to come. Paul declares in verse 11, He who raised Christ from the dead will give life to your mortal bodies through His Spirit who lives in you. Easter proclaims that Jesus holds full power over our eventual graves too." After a pause, I transitioned into the following story:

> Norena lived in South Florida. When Hurricane Andrew struck in 1992, her home was one of many that was severely damaged. The elderly woman received an insurance settlement, and the repair work began. However, when the money ran out, the contractor left too. Without money to finish the repair work, Norena got by with just a small lamp and a single burner. No air conditioning. No hot showers. No refrigerated food. Yet the real tragedy here ... is that Norena continued to live like this for 15 more years! Long after the power had been restored in her community, Norena continued to live in her dark, unfinished home. Finally, after acting on a tip, the mayor of Miami-Dade got involved, and within a few hours, Norena had electricity again. CBS News reported that Norena planned to let the water get really hot and take her first bubble bath in a decade and a half.
>
> What a tragedy! All the power that Norena needed was right there. She just needed to be connected; she just needed to be plugged in. Her story reminds me of an even greater misfortune today. The tomb is empty. The crucified is risen. Jesus lives! All the power that we need for forgiveness and eternal life is there. It's present. It's available. It's free. And yet people all over this world continue to live in spiritual darkness—not connected to Jesus—and many for much longer than 15 years. (Pause)
>
> How about you? Are you connected? He is risen! The power of Easter abounds for you. Have you been plugged in? Do you believe in Jesus as your risen Lord and Savior? Have you been baptized into His Name? If you answer Yes, then praise God, the Holy Spirit has already connected you to the power of Easter and its benefits for eternity. If you're not sure, but you are open to hearing more

about Jesus, please, I'd love to talk with you after the service. I also invite you to consider coming to Discovery Class next week. There you can ask any questions you'd like. You'll learn more about Jesus and how you can unleash the unstoppable power of Easter in your life. By God's grace and for His glory. He is risen! (He is risen, indeed! Alleluia!) Amen. Let's pray.

Pulling a Loop
Another homiletical maneuver deserves mention as well: the preacher pulls a full-loop or a vertical 360 with the sermon. This move is also deemed an *inclusio*. In other words, the homilist opens with a story or scenario that leaves the hearers suspended. Then, after expounding the text, he returns full-loop to the opening story or scenario to offer a resolution that exemplifies the main thrust of the text. "Pulling a loop" can be used with either direct or connecting-flight sermon structures. Here is an example from John 14:1-3.

> Several years ago George Tulloch set out on a quest to raise a 16'x24' section of the Titanic that had broken off from the hull as it sank 2.5 miles below the Atlantic to the ocean floor. The piece weighed 20 tons and was buried in ocean muck. Special submarines were able to go down to that section of the hull, attach six balloons to it, and fill those balloons with diesel fuel. Large pulleys on Tulloch's ship began to slowly wench the 20-ton piece from the ocean floor. Yet on the 2.5-mile journey to the surface, the wind and waves picked up. Tulloch's vessel was ordered not to try to tow the piece towards the shore. Sure enough, under the added stress of the waves, all six ropes began to fray. When the 16'x24' section came within 70 yards of the surface, the ropes broke, and that section of hull sank back to the ocean floor. You can imagine the heavy hearts on Tulloch's ship that day. (Pause) Today's text opens in the same way, with some very heavy hearts.
>
> I. Three reasons why Jesus's disciples had heavy hearts (14:1).
>   a. One of them was going to betray Jesus (13:21).
>   b. Jesus would soon be leaving them (13:33).
>   c. Jesus said Peter would deny Him three times (13:38).

II. Reasons why we have troubled hearts.
   a. Be specific.
   b. Be specific.
III. Jesus points us beyond the burdens of this world to the Father's house.
   a. The Father's house has ample space for everyone. (v. 2a)
   b. Our rooms are being constructed by Jesus, the Carpenter-God! (v. 2b)
   c. Jesus promises, "I'm coming back to take you there." (v. 3)

That disheartening day, as the piece from the Titanic sank back to the ocean floor, George Tulloch went to his cabin, made a sign, and hung it over the rail of the ship for his crew to see. It read: "I will come back. George Tulloch." Two years later, George Tulloch successfully retrieved that 20-ton piece from the ocean floor. How much more does Jesus leave us with that same pledge today! Jesus promises, Jesus guarantees: "If I go and prepare a place for you, *I will come back* and take you, that where I am, you also may be. I will come back. I promise." With such comfort lavished on our hearts, we hope in and we anticipate His imminent return. Think about it: even today, we're that much closer to home. Amen.

An Afterword from the Cockpit

In case you are wondering, my dad loved airplanes. He flew Cessna 152s and 172s when we were young, and our house had no shortage of airplane books, models, or toys. In fact, when dad heard a jet or helicopter fly over our house, he ran outside to see what it was. He even drove our family to airports just to watch planes take off and land. One year, we spent our entire family vacation at the annual airshow in Oshkosh, Wisconsin, where *everyone* is "plane" crazy. And talk about *worry*, I used to dread when dad would fly the Cessna several thousand feet in the air and do a *stall*. If you know flying, you know exactly what I'm talking about. Why stall a perfectly running engine?!!!

Additionally, I thank Captain David B. for his help with some technical wording in this chapter. Captain B. flies Boeing 777s around the world; he even shared this chapter with two co-pilots to solicit their feedback as well. I am most grateful for their time, insight, and encouragement.

CHAPTER 10

Panning for Gold: Using Illustrations

Although I have never "panned for gold" in the literal sense, this aspect of sermon preparation and delivery seems to favor one extreme or the other. For instance, when the illustration needle is pegged to the right, illustrations are overused and abused. Story after story cloud the text. Conversely, when the illustration needle is pegged to the left, homilies resemble long and lifeless lectures. Words, sentences, and paragraphs blur together, and hearers yearn for the homily to end (i.e, the final "amen"). Somewhere in the middle, however, a sweet spot exists where an opportune illustration—much like a silver platter—bears a luscious hors d'oeuvre of biblical truth. Or, put another way, timely illustrations are not the gems themselves, but the casings—the delivery system—that house the most precious jewel: scriptural truth.

Illustrating Illustrations
The best discourse for understanding illustrations in preaching comes from Charles Haddon Spurgeon (1834-1892). Spurgeon compares sermon illustrations to a house with windows:

> Windows greatly add to the pleasure and agreeableness of a habitation, and so do *illustrations make a sermon pleasurable and interesting*. A building without windows would be a prison

rather than a house, for it would be quite dark ... in the same way, a discourse without a parable is prosy and dull, and involves a grievous weariness of the flesh... No reason exists why the preaching of the gospel should be a miserable operation either to the speaker or to the hearer. Pleasantly profitable let all our sermons be. A house must not have thick walls without openings, neither must a discourse be all made up of solid slabs of doctrine without a window of comparison or a lattice of poetry... Every architect will tell you that he looks upon his windows *as an opportunity for introducing ornament into his design.* A pile may be massive, but it cannot be pleasing if it is not broken up with windows and other details... Sermons need to be broken up, varied, decorated, and enlivened; and nothing can do this so well as the introduction of types, emblems, and instances.[1]

Spurgeon adds,

Illustrations tend to enliven an audience and quicken attention. Windows, when they will open ... are a great blessing by refreshing and reviving the audience... While we thus commend illustrations for necessary uses, it must be remembered that they are not the strength of a sermon any more than a window is the strength of a house; and for this reason, among others, *they should not be too numerous.* Too many openings for light may seriously detract from the stability of a building... *Illustrations should really cast light upon the subject in hand,* otherwise they are sham windows, and all shams are an abomination... Jesus must be all in all; his gospel must be the beginning and end of all our discoursing; parable and poesy must be under his feet, and eloquence must wait upon him as his servant. The best light comes in through the clearest glass.[2]

While windows allow light into a house but are not load-bearing

---

[1] Charles Haddon Spurgeon, *Lectures to My Students* (Grand Rapids: Baker Book House, 1977 [1894]), Third Series, Lecture 1, 1-13, as quoted in Richard Lischer, ed., *The Company of Preachers: Wisdom on Preaching, Augustine to the Present* (Grand Rapids: William B. Eerdmans Publishing Company, 2002), 317-18.

[2] Ibid., 318-22.

structures, so illustrations shed light on biblical truth. However, illustrations must never bear the weight of the sermon; rather, the text stands as the main support beam for the entire homiletical structure.

Biblical Precedent
As we discuss the need for illustrations in preaching, the question looms: does biblical precedent exist for the use of stories, illustrations, and analogies in the pulpit? Consider the following:

> The LORD sent Nathan to David ... and said to him, "There were two men in a certain city, the one rich and the other poor... Now there came a traveler to the rich man, and he was unwilling to take one of his own flock or herd to prepare for the guest who had come to him, but he took the poor man's lamb and prepared it for the man who had come to him."... Nathan said to David, 'You are the man [who did this]!'" (2 Sam 12:1-7).

God sends the prophet Nathan with an illustration in hand to confront David's sin with Bathsheba. So also, David proclaims on the day the LORD rescued him from his enemies and the hand of Saul, "The LORD is my rock and my fortress and my deliverer, my God, my rock, in whom I take refuge, my shield, and the horn of my salvation, my stronghold" (Ps 18:2). In one verse David paints eight powerful word-pictures of God—a mural of hope, safety, and deliverance for God's people. Likewise, Isaiah prophesies how God had "a vineyard on a very fertile hill. He dug it and cleared it of stones, and planted it with choice vines... He looked for it to make grapes, but it made wild grapes" (Isa 5:1-2).[3] Similarly, God directs Jeremiah: "Go, buy a potter's earthenware flask... Then you shall break the flask in the sight of the men who go with you, and you shall say to them, 'Thus says the LORD of hosts: So I will break this people and this city, as one breaks a potter's vessel, so that it can never be mended" (Jer 19:1, 10-11). These passages evidence the illustrative teaching that spans the genres of the

---

3 The literal translation of the Hebrew text for *be'ushim* would be "stinking things" or even "stench fruit." Francis Brown, S. R. Driver, and Charles A. Briggs, *The Brown-Driver-Briggs Hebrew and English Lexicon* (Peabody, MA: Hendrickson Publishers, 2000), 93.

First Testament.

Jesus utilizes stories, analogies, parables, and first century images in His preaching and teaching too. He taps commonalities such as agriculture, sheep, fish, banquets, laborers, temple, investors, currency, and treasure to illustrate and illumine divine truth. Take, for instance, Jesus's words: "You are the salt of the earth... You are the light of the world... Why do you see the speck that is in your brother's eye, but do not notice the log that is in your own eye? Or how can you say to your brother, 'Let me take the speck out of your eye,' when there is the log in your own eye?" (Matt 5:13-14; 7:3-5). Ian Macpherson guesstimates that the illustrative ratio in Jesus's teaching approaches 75 percent.[4] In fact, in the midst of speaking seven parables, Matthew adds, "All these things Jesus said to the crowds in parables; indeed, *he said nothing to them without a parable*" (Matt 13:34). Jesus's exclusive use of parables to the crowds—teaching that must be decoded for understanding—actually fulfills First Testament prophecy (cf. Isa 6:9-10; Matt 13:14-15). Jesus's explicit use of illustrative teaching and preaching functions as messianic signifiers for His true identity, meaning even Jesus's hortatory proclaims His messiahship.

Paul employs illustrative oration in his public ministry as well. In Romans 12 and 1 Corinthians 12, Paul compares the church to a human body; each spiritually gifted and indispensable person or part contributes to the whole. In Ephesians 6, Paul likens believers' spiritual warfare to the armor and preparedness of a Roman soldier. Elsewhere Paul applies athletic imagery to impart divine truth. In Corinthians 9, he associates Christians with Olympic runners who compete for the prize; and in 1 Timothy 6 and 2 Timothy 4, he equates the Christian faith with stepping into a boxing ring.

Peter describes Satan as a prowling, roaring lion who hunts believers (1 Pet 5:8). The church can trust Peter's alarm; he speaks from first-hand experience with the evil one (Luke 22:54-62). Jesus even warned Peter beforehand that Satan had demanded to sift him as wheat (Luke

---

4 Ian MacPherson, *The Art of Illustrating Sermons* (Nashville: Abingdon, 1964), cited in Chapell, *Christ-Centered Preaching*, 189.

22:31)—another powerful image in Scripture.[5] Likewise, the apostle John (suffering tribulation and exile on Patmos) describes Satan as "a furious, great red dragon" who—failing to triumph over Jesus—has declared war on the church militant (Rev 12:3-17).

Throughout both Testaments, God indirectly (via prophets and apostles) and directly conveys His word to ordinary people using conventional imagery and shared experience. These vivid and meaningful pictures capture hearts and minds as the Spirit works repentance, faith, and obedience through the preached Word. As a result, the biblical precedent for graphic, visually-oriented preaching has been given to assist, direct, and inspire illustrative preaching in pulpits today.

Wisdom for Illustrating

Having examined the need, function, and precedent for illustrative preaching, it is time to establish a few basic "rules" (i.e., expositional wisdom) for selecting and using illustrative material in sermons.

- **Start with a text, not an illustration:** The temptation exists when an expositor comes across a powerful—even funny—illustration or story to begin one's sermon planning there. It follows, then, that the homilist scans Scripture for a passage to prop up his story or illustration. God's Word, however, must drive the sermon, never illustrative content. Safeguard Scripture as the rightful foundation for every homily and keep illustrations—as good as they may be—subservient to the text.
- **Spiritualize the illustration, not the text:** Let's face it, spiritualizing Scripture—particularly historical and gospel narrative—is enticing because it preaches with little effort. Spiritualizing Scripture sounds like the following: *Which "Mount Sinai" is God calling you to summit so that He can reveal Himself to you? What "Jordan River" is God calling you to cross, even if it feels like flood stage right now, so that He can bring you to His desired "Promised Land"? Which "wall of Jericho" is God calling you to march around so that He can crumble that obstacle in your*

---

[5] Interestingly, when Jesus warns, "Satan demanded to have you, that he might sift you like wheat," both *you-s* are plural in Greek, meaning not just Peter, but all of Jesus's disciples were targets. Hence, Peter charges every believer to stand on guard in faith and resist the evil beast (1 Pet 5:9).

faith-walk with Him? My friend, this is Exegetical Fallacy 101![6] Not only does spiritualizing Scripture misuse and misapply texts, but it is hardly the author's intent or purpose either.

Rather, spiritualize illustrations. For instance, when preaching on Ephesians 4:29-30 and the destructive power of words, I spiritualized the following illustration:

> Many of you probably remember the TV show Myth Busters, the show that paired urban legend with scientific testing. The producers concede that their biggest mishap occurred in 2011 in Dublin, CA. The crew built their own cannon and intended to fire a live cannonball through three large drums of colored water. The shot, however, missed, and the cantaloupe-sized ball ripped through a backstop, skipped off a hillside, flew 700 yards in the air, smashed through a resident's front door, raced up their stairs, blasted out their bedroom wall, crossed a six-lane road, took off several roofing tiles from another house, and finally came to rest in a minivan that had just been parked five minutes earlier. Amazingly, not one person was injured as the cannonball ripped through the community and left a path of destruction in its wake.
>
> Our tongues wield the same power, don't they? Our words—like reckless cannonballs—fly from our lips and rip through homes, families, marriages, workplaces, and congregations, and they leave a wake of internal destruction and damage behind. Our words can even be deadly. That's why Paul says in our text today, "Let no corrupting talk come out of your mouths." (Eph 4:29). The Greek word for corrupting is *sapros*. Jesus uses the same word in Luke 6:43 for "rotten fruit" and in Matthew 13:48 for "rotten fish." Literally, Paul has in mind, "Let no rotten, foul-smelling, reeking talk come out of your mouths"; the damage will always be great, even deadly.

---

6 A most helpful resource on exegetical integrity in preaching and teaching is D. A. Carson, *Exegetical Fallacies*, 2nd ed. (Grand Rapids: Baker Academic, 2006).

- **Put the time in:** Panning for gold requires considerable patience. Gold prospectors must carefully sift through myriads of gravel to reveal nuggets or shavings. In this way, finding quality, illustrative material can be compared to panning for gold. Shortcuts do not exist. However, once the preacher finds a golden nugget, the illustration can "open a window" on the text and bring biblical truth—the real gold—to light. Conversely, telling illustrations for illustrations' sake offers your people nothing more than fool's gold.

On average, I spend one to two hours per sermon filtering through scores (sometimes hundreds) of potential illustrations. My go-to resource is www.preachingtoday.com. The annual membership fee is reasonable, and I can search for illustrative material by Scripture reference, topic, or key word. I can also narrow the field by selecting preferences such as quotes, humor, stories, props and symbols, statistics, tone, audience type, and source. For example, I just typed "anger" in *Preaching Today*'s search box and 311 illustrations surfaced. Now I must pan them for gold.

As you can imagine, the sources for illustrations appear endless. They could be found on the internet, books, digital media, everyday life, nature, etc. Sometimes a simple Google search can net results. Keep an eye on your local newspaper too; it can highlight concerns in your community (i.e., in your congregation's backyard). To assist your hunt for illustrative content, first try to plan out your preaching calendar by major topic, series, or theme at least six to twelve months prior. This technique heightens your vision for potential material far in advance. Second, organize illustrations in a way that works for you. Though I have three filing systems for illustrations (alphabetical by topic, upcoming sermons, and specific sermon occasions), I primarily use the latter two. For "upcoming sermons," if I see a promising illustration, story, or statistic, I print it as soon as possible and tuck it in the appropriate folder for fast, future reference. For "specific sermon occasions," I have individual folders marked Christmas Eve, New Years, Epiphany, Ash Wednesday, Palm Sunday, Maundy Thursday, Good Friday, Easter, Ascension,

Pentecost, Trinity, Mother's Day, Father's Day, 4th of July, Rally Day, Reformation, Thanksgiving, Weddings, Funerals, Graduation, Church Anniversary, Ordination/Installation, Stewardship, etc. Thus, when I come across a potential hit (or fit), I file it accordingly—especially for critical sermons such as Christmas Eve and Easter when many in culture still come to us! So, organize and hunt. Hunt and organize. Sifting requires time, but the homiletical payoff is golden!

- **Think visual and stay visual:** It's no secret that we live in a visual society; humanity has been inundated with screens. We have screens in pockets, cars, kitchens, bedrooms, breakrooms, sanctuaries, fitness centers, restaurants, supermarkets, gas pumps—even on our wrists! Nielsen Company reports that the average American intakes 10 hours and 39 minutes of media per day ... and growing![7] America runs on visual overdrive. Side effects include decreased attention span and increased boredom. One study of 2,000 participants in North America (Canada) revealed that the average attention span has fallen from 12 seconds in 2000 to just 8 seconds in 2015—a shorter attention span than the average goldfish (9 seconds).[8] Obviously, the more preachers can keep it visual in the pulpit the better; however, because preaching is not a show, do not confuse visual and engaging with entertaining. Rather, visual assistance in the pulpit can take the form of PowerPoint or Keynote slides; sermon props; appropriate body motions or gestures; word-pictures from the text; accompanying graphics on fill-in-the-blank sermon notes; a brief skit or narrative reenactment, etc. The precedent has already been established in both Testaments, and we have the added benefit of special lighting, sound, and digital HD, among other subservient effects.

---

7 "Americans Devote More than 10 Hours a Day to Screen Time, and Growing," *CNN*, July 29, 2016, accessed June 14, 2018, https://www.cnn.com/2016/06/30/health/americans-screen-time-nielsen/index.html.

8 "Humans Have Shorter Attention Spans than Goldfish, Thanks to Smartphones," *The Telegraph*, May 15, 2015, accessed June 14, 2018, https://www.telegraph.co.uk/science/2016/03/12/humans-have-shorter-attention-span-than-goldfish-thanks-to-smart.

- **Get permission beforehand**: The longer a pastor serves a congregation, the more personal their relationships grow. Pastor and flock do life together, including peaks and valleys. Consequently, referencing personal stories from the community of believers can be a powerful instrument in preaching. Paul commends more than 26 exemplar believers to the church in Rome (Rom 16:1-16), as well as Timothy and Epaphroditus to the saints in Philippi (Phil 2:19-30). By the Spirit's continuous work, examples of textual faithfulness and obedience abound in parishes today. Some stories bear witness to fidelity in times of hardship and suffering, while other stories model humbleness in times of wellness and plenty.

  Before sharing from someone's life, however, the loving, sensitive, and prudent first step is to receive their blessing *in a timely manner* beforehand, never post-sermon. In a HIPAA and identity-sensitive culture, a heightened awareness exists to protect personal information. Even in church we want to honor people's privacy, avoid assumptions, and preclude any unnecessary harm to the sheep. Therefore, when seeking permission to share from someone's life—whether a time of faithfulness or on rare occasions a faith-lesson from disobedience—be open, clear, compassionate, gentle, honest, and specific about your intention and train-of-thought with their story. When in doubt, err on the side of caution. If permission is denied, affirm the individual and be delicate with their "no." Do not push or prod for a "yes." Furthermore, if their story broaches a sensitive issue, it might be a good idea to write out your exact words for that portion of the sermon and seek their final blessing prior to delivery. And preacher, please heed this advice too: ask your wife and children for permission before sharing from your familial life. Again, never assume. Their privacy and comfort level for congregational exposure matters as well! Lastly, though we do not have to ask permission to share stories and examples from our personal life and walk with the Lord, let us keep them modest and far apart, lest we appear conceited or limited in our week-to-week sermon material.

What about Humor?

Opinions vary widely regarding the use of humor in preaching, especially the telling of jokes or funny stories.[9] Valid concerns exist on both sides of the debate. Those who oppose humorous illustrations in preaching cite concerns such as deep reverence for the Word; the dignity of the pastoral office; and the impression of preaching as comedy. Those who endorse humor in the pulpit express the sincere desire to connect with congregants on a human level; to arrest and hold hearer attention; as well as to springboard into textual truth. If used tactfully, appropriately, and sporadically, jokes and funny stories can be assets in preaching. However, a preacher should refrain from telling jokes if the humor does not serve the text or lead hearers into the overarching theme. In addition, though biblical truth is never a joking matter, sometimes dipping a hard or convicting truth in a dab of humor "helps the medicine go down."

When our congregation launched a sermon series "[Road] Signs of Lent" (i.e., U-Turn, Yield, Cross-road, One Way, etc.),[10] I used the following humor to segway into the entire series on road signs:

> A state trooper was parked on the side of a highway watching for speeders. A car traveling 22mph grabbed his attention. Considering the vehicle as dangerous as a speeder, he quickly turned on his lights and pulled the car over. As the officer approached the vehicle, he noticed five elderly ladies inside—two in the front seat and three in back. Confused, the driver said to the officer: "I don't understand, sir, I was going the exact speed limit. What seems to be the problem?" Holding back a chuckle, the officer kindly explained that 22 was the route number, not the speed limit. Embarrassed, the elderly driver apologized and thanked him for his sincerity. Before the officer let her go though, he inquired, "Are you other ladies okay? You look a little pale." "Oh, they're fine," said the driver, "we were just on Route 119."[11]

---

[9] An elderly pastor once told me: "I didn't tell funny stories in the pulpit; I told stories funny. There's a difference between the two." Interview with Charles Mueller Sr., June 6, 2018.

[10] The Lenten sermon series was inspired by a worship kit from *Creative Communications for the Parish*. We purchased the kit and made the series our own.

[11] I simply Googled a joke about road signs and this one grabbed my attention. After I said this joke, every hearer was tuned in for what I had to say next.

Needless to say, I had every hearer's attention as I introduced the series and transitioned into the text.

Golden Nuggets

In an Easter sermon on the sting of death being removed (1 Cor 15:50-56), I used the following illustration to transition into the conclusion and drive the intended function of the text home:

> A couple of years ago I woke up early one morning and noticed something out the kitchen window. I had never seen this before; a possum was darting around our backyard. One, I couldn't believe it: I was witnessing a live possum. Previously, I had only seen roadkill or at least "playing roadkill." And two, I was shocked at how fast the rodent moved! He (or she) was here, there, and gone in no time.
>
> But you know, I remember reading a few years ago that possums are actually pretty smart animals. I read that if a possum walks up to a hole and sees only one set of tracks going in, it will not enter the hole because it knows that something else is still down there. However, if a possum notices two sets of tracks near the hole—one set leading in and one set leading out—it walks straight in because it knows that the hole is vacant. There is nothing to fear.
>
> How much more the baptized of Jesus Christ! The sting of death has been removed! There is still an empty tomb in Israel to this day proclaiming the resurrection of Jesus from the dead. Because of this day some 2,000 years ago, we can face death ... we can enter our graves without fear ... because there is a second set of tracks coming out on Easter morning! ... Alleluia, Christ is risen! He is risen, indeed!

In a sermon on John 10:1-18, I opened with the question:

> "If you could be any animal in the world for one day, what would you be?" I encouraged the worshipers to share with those sitting around them. At the contemporary service, I asked people to

volunteer their answers when I called on them (children included). I followed up: isn't that something, no one said they'd want to be a sheep, yet of all the animals in the world to choose from, in the Bible, God likens us to sheep. Baaaa! Why is that? Why sheep?

Later in the same sermon I told this story as I referenced Isaiah 53:6:

I read about a group of shepherds in Gevas, Turkey. As they were enjoying breakfast together, one of their 1,500 sheep decided to jump off a nearby cliff and plummet to its death. Guess what happened next? The rest of the sheep began to jump too. The Aksam newspaper reported that 450 sheep died that day; thankfully the fluffy pile of wool at the bottom began to pad the other sheep as they fell. Though it wasn't a total loss that day, their estimated financial loss topped $100,000 in a country where the average person makes less than $3,000 a year.[12]

Isaiah speaks of a similar fate. We all like sheep have gone astray; each one of us has turned to our own way. On our own we wander into all kinds of sin—lusting and lying, slander and stealing, cursing and coveting—each sin powerful enough to plunge us to eternal death and destruction.

In a sermon from Proverbs 5 on marital faithfulness, I employed the following illustration:

It's amazing what we—especially men—can learn from male turkeys on marital faithfulness. Male turkeys, often referred to as toms or gobblers, are created with a unique ability. When a tom gobbles, a hen within range will answer his call and move toward him. During the spring mating season, a tom might call for potential mates all day long. There is one exception though. If a tom already has a hen with him, most of the time he will not leave his girl to check out another potential mate, no matter how enticing her response feels. Again, a tom is wired to know that the

---

[12] Adapted from https://www.preachingtoday.com/search/?query=Gevas.

female comes to him. In most cases, a mature tom will not leave the hen he can see to chase down a hen that he cannot see. It's against his nature. But every once and a while, a tom will violate everything he knows to be true and leave his hen for another. But what sounded like another willing mate was actually a hunter staring down the barrel of a loaded gun. Bang![13] The temptation was deadly; the tom never came home. Gentlemen, husbands, fiancées, boyfriends ... what seems so innocent, a glance here and there, a little innocent flirting ... is enough lust to prove deadly. Therefore verse 15 bids us, "Drink water from your own cistern, flowing water from your own well." Friends in Christ, the grass is not greener on the other side, but where it's watered most.

In a sermon on Philippians 2:1-4, I spoke about how pride affects us all. I then shared the following study on human brains:

Have you ever been really excited about a recent purchase or bonus at work? Have you ever savored a tender steak or a slice of peanut butter pie? You know that Mmmm moment of satisfaction. A few years ago, neuroscientists at Harvard University monitored human brain activity and discovered this about ourselves: when we talk about ourselves—whether in a personal conversation or through social media sites—Facebook, Twitter, Snapchat—the same area of our brains lights up ... begins to fire rapidly ... as when we delight in food or money ... Mmmm. Pizza ... Mmmm. Hot fudge brownies ... Mmmm. Purchasing a new car or clothing ... Mmmm. Talking and posting about ourselves ... Mmmm. It's rewarding. It feels great, doesn't it? This study explains why, on average, we devote 40% of everyday conversation and media use to talking about ourselves.[14] Mmmmm.

Isn't that something? Our sinful nature is so bent on ourselves, that even our innermost brain cells and synapses like us. Yet Paul

---

13 Adapted from https://www.preachingtoday.com/search/?query=Turkey&type=.
14 "Science Reveals Why We Brag So Much," Wall Street Journal, May 7, 2012, accessed June 18, 2018, https://www.wsj.com/articles/SB10001424052702304451104577390392329291890.

says in our text today: "In humility count others more significant than yourselves. Let each of you look not only to his own interests, but also to the interests of others." Paul directs us outward—not just in our actions, but even in our thoughts and with our tongues.

Finally, I want to leave you with two illustrations or images that I have used from the original languages to shed light on their respective texts.

In Genesis 2:24, God defines His blueprint for marriage: "Therefore a man shall leave his father and his mother and hold fast to his wife, and they shall become one flesh." What does it mean for a man to *hold fast* to his wife? The Hebrew word for "hold fast" is *dabaq*. Its use elsewhere in Scripture paints a powerful picture for spouses. Dabaq means "to hold fast" or "cleave to," and it's used in the Bible for a soldier's hand holding fast to his sword. It's used for a tongue which clings to the roof of a parched mouth; and it's used of human flesh cleaving to the bone. In other words, "holding fast" in marriage conveys the picture of permanence. (Pause) Within weeks of moving into our new house in Chicagoland, our youngest son broke the latch off from our aluminum gate. I tried Super Glue; I tried Lock-tite—neither lasted for a day. Then I went to a hardware store and came home with an epoxy that bonds metal to metal ... the latch hasn't budged. It continues to dabaq, to hold fast, to cleave—one piece to another, the latch to its post. Such permanence, such bonding, is God's blueprint for marriage too.

In Philippians 4:5b-7, believers are promised: "The Lord is at hand; do not be anxious about anything, but in everything by prayer and supplication with thanksgiving let your requests be made known to God. And the peace of God, which surpasses all understanding, *will guard* your hearts and your minds in Christ Jesus." The Greek word for "will guard" is *phroureo*, and it literally means "to post an armed garrison of soldiers around."[15] Given Paul's beating and

---

15 Gordon D. Fee, *Paul's Letter to the Philippians*, NICNT (Grand Rapids: Eerdmans Publishing Company, 1995), 411.

imprisonment in Philippi (Acts 16), believers there would readily connect with this word-image in his letter. Yet rather than being anxious about what awaited them in prison, Paul and Silas spent the first night of incarceration praying and praising God. Not only did God's peace surround their hearts and minds like a garrison of armed soldiers, but God utilized a "jail house rock" to open wide their cells and to loosen their chains. (Pause) Friends, when troubles abound, we can be anxious, or we can pray. We have God's promise that when we give everything to God in prayer and leave it there with Him, His perfect peace—like a detachment of elite soldiers—will guard our hearts and minds in Christ Jesus.

CHAPTER 11

Top 10 Odds and Ends of Preaching

The Top 10 Signs You Might Be a Preacher
10. You won a church raffle and members complained it was rigged.
9. You went to Dairy Queen and asked for a church split.
8. You named your boat "Collection Plate."
7. You dreamed you were preaching only to realize that you were.
6. You're leading your flock into the 21st century but don't know what you're preaching on next Sunday.
5. The congregation mounted a clock in the pulpit.
4. You wish your deacons would drench you with Gatorade after a killer sermon.
3. You wanted to fire the church and form a congregation search committee.
2. You're very responsible—if something goes wrong, you're responsible.
1. You'd pick jury duty over another wedding.

From time-to-time I enjoy giving "Top 10s" in my preaching and teaching, such as "The Top 10 Signs You Might Be a Veteran Mom" or "The Top 10 Signs You Might Be a Lutheran." In a similar way, I offer you "Top 10 Odds and Ends" of preaching that can bless your pulpit ministry. In no order of importance:

1. **Be yourself.** In an age of instant access to many gifted, published, and popular preachers, the pressure can be immense to emulate someone in our own preaching—even borrow sermons from them. I am not espousing that we shouldn't learn from other preachers to improve our own homiletical methods or delivery. Neither am I saying that we cannot recycle a textual point or illustration that we hear, but in a culture that values authenticity, integrity compels us to be who God has made us—both in and out of the pulpit. So, void of narcissistic implications, be you.

2. **Try something new.** If you feel your preaching could be settling into a rut, converse with trusted leaders in your congregation. Do others sense it too? It could just be your own insecurity or anxiety. Either way, try something new from time-to-time. A sudden or unexpected change-up in preaching can keep routineness in check. Use a sermon prop. Add an accompanying PowerPoint or Keynote. If you use the pulpit, try stepping out of it, even for a minute or two. If you walk around and preach, deliver all or part of your message while sitting on a high stool. As long as "the something new" is appropriate and does not *detract* or *distract* from the text, then why not? Again, your leadership can offer constructive feedback (my wife and children provide "mostly constructive" feedback too!).

3. **Practice your delivery.** If delivering a sermon is just as important as the time we devote to praying, planning, and preparing it, do we rehearse the message for maximum flow, poise, and effectiveness? Preparation and delivery are not an either-or, but a both-and. Great delivery, minus adequate preparation time, equals a sermon with the depth of a kiddie pool. Conversely, time poured into sermon preparation without attention to delivery is as good as scuba gear without fins; we're fit to go deep, but progress will be slow and choppy.

    When I was a vicar (student pastor), I practiced each sermon five to six times from the pulpit. Fifteen years later, I still need to run through each sermon two to three times in my head. For Christmas Eve and Easter, I often practice the sermon once or twice "live" (in the actual sanctuary) to achieve maximum delivery.

Hence, from inception to delivery, I average twelve to fifteen hours per homily; wedding and funeral sermons average two to three hours each. What does that look like? Monday mornings I block out four hours for prayer, translation, word studies, commentaries, stating the intended meaning, and noting any homiletical ideas that come to mind. If time permits, I gather potential illustrations too. On Thursdays I block out six hours to review Monday's notes; create a working outline; type up fill-in-the-blank sermon notes (if a connecting flight structure); fill out one of the ½-page sermon notes (complete with illustrations) to use as my final preaching outline; and create an accompanying Keynote (if applicable). On Saturdays I run through the full sermon outline two to three times in my head.

Do we have numerous and varying weekly responsibilities in ministry? Absolutely! Personally, however, I always come back to Acts 6:2b-4: "It is not right that we should give up preaching the word of God to serve tables ... we will devote ourselves to prayer and to the ministry of the word." Though these words of Scripture are *descriptive* rather than *prescriptive*, the text implies an emphasis on preaching and prayer in pastoral ministry.

4. **Record and review your delivery.** As preachers, it is important to review our own "game film" from time-to-time, even though it can be awkward and uncomfortable. However, look for the following habits: Do we talk too fast? Do we pause long enough and at proper times? Do we signal transitions to our hearers or jump track and hope they follow? Do we overuse hand motions or notice any distracting body gestures? Do we maintain sufficient eye contact, or are we overly dependent on notes or a manuscript? If we walk around during the sermon, does our movement appear natural? Do we tend to favor one side of the congregation during delivery? Do our pace, inflection, tone of voice, and appearance complement the message? Record. Review. Adjust. Repeat. We might notice aspects of our preaching or personal tendencies of which we were completely unaware.

5. **Plan an annual or bi-annual homiletical retreat.** Impress upon your leaders that this two- to three-day retreat is not a weekend

getaway or a vacation; rather, it's consecrated time for prayer, for mulling over Scripture and the needs of the flock, and for planning out the next six to twelve months of the homiletical calendar. If your regular practice is lectionary preaching, you can begin to pour over texts and highlight weekly themes. You might even notice an epistle or gospel unit that you could create a five- to six-week series around. If your regular practice is crafting sermon series, then jot down potential series that correlate with the spiritual needs of the people, as well as potential series for Advent, the New Year, Lent, post-Easter, and the summer months. If you have a preaching staff, take them with you. Not only does a homiletical retreat sharpen your own focus and give direction moving forward, but communicating the upcoming topics and themes benefits your worship planning, music ministry, website content, and small groups ministry too.

6. **Listen to other preachers.** "Iron sharpens iron, and one man sharpens another" (Prov 27:17). One way that clergy can sharpen and be sharpened as preachers is by listening to other homilists in the field. Countless sermons are readily available on the internet; extinct are the days of having to stockpile cassettes and CDs in the center console of your car. Seminaries post chapel sermons. Congregations upload weekly messages. Block out an hour each week to just listen, observe, learn, and be fed. Journal any thoughts or ideas that surface. A few clergy from my D.Min. cohort have a set time each week when they gather online, view a sermon together, and reflect on the style, content, and presentation. Perhaps you could form an online community too.

7. **Take a weekly Sabbath and regular vacation time.** Jesus sent the apostles out in pairs to do ministry in His authority. When the apostles returned and told Him all that they had done and taught, Jesus commanded them, "'Come away by yourselves to a desolate place and rest a while.' For many were coming and going, and they had no leisure even to eat" (Mark 6:31). As Jesus molds the first generation of church leaders, ministry detachment and rest are not optional or an afterthought. Jesus understands the tension between human limitations and endless ministry demands. He created us human beings, not "human doings,"

and preachers are not exempt.

Thus, take (and model) a weekly Sabbath. Separate. Rest. Refresh. Re-engage. Self-care is biblical. Paul charges young pastor Timothy: "Give *close attention to yourself* and to the teaching" (1 Tim 4:16a, author's translation). "To yourself" embraces more than Timothy's doctrine; it includes his personal well-being for public ministry too. How can we preach spiritual, physical, emotional, mental, marital, and familial wellness if we are not exemplifying it ourselves? Too many pastors endorse "ministry polygamy": they court their spouse *and* their congregation. The church already has a Husband, and it is not the guy in the pulpit. The Bridegroom paid a steep price for her; He's the head of this marital union. The Bride will be just fine if pastors limit themselves to 5-5½ days per week. Besides, I quickly learned that it takes a full day just to help my spouse and family attend to the house, yard, vehicles, groceries, errands, and appointments. However, "help around the house days" do not count as Sabbath (i.e., spiritual and mental rest) for the preacher. Sorry!

Take regular vacations too. "The laborer deserves his wages," including his accrued vacation time (1 Tim 5:18). When you prioritize systematic separation and rest, you recharge your preaching as well. God established a *divine order* for public ministry. Paul instructs Timothy: "[An overseer] must manage his own household well, with all dignity keeping his children submissive, for if someone does not know how to manage his own household, how will he care for God's church?" (1 Tim 3:4-5). Brother, which household comes first—God's or yours? Good management *in your home* is the prerequisite for God's: MASTER – MATE – MINISTRY ... in that respective order. Healthy home management requires significant time, energy, focus, effort, and sacrifice.

Finally, no persons—including preachers—are immortal or irreplaceable. So, how are you setting up or not setting up a healthy ministry environment for the preacher (and his family!) who will follow you? Do you ponder that? Ask yourself: "How can I make the ministry here (boundaries included) even better for the next pastor and for his family?" At a minimum, set the precedent for weekly Sabbaths and time away!

8. **Use seasons of "low tide" to prepare for "high tide."** I currently serve a parish with a parochial school. September through May are happening months. While summer provides a much-needed slowdown for staff, summer also provides pivotal time to work and plan ahead. Granted, ministry will always have changing tides—including an occasional hurricane or tsunami. Yet Scripture summons us to look to the ant: "Consider her ways, and be wise. Without having any chief, officer, or ruler, she prepares her bread in summer and gathers her food in harvest" (Prov 6:6-7). Where can your ministry learn from the ant?

9. **Invest in good commentaries.** God has blessed His church with exceptional scholarship. Digital media, computer programs, and online databases have revolutionized research, print, and availability. The volumes of resources and books that clergy have access to is unparalleled. Though most personal libraries come with a price, the weekly payout—especially for preaching—vastly outweighs the expense. Set a goal of two reputable commentaries per book of the Bible. Though you may want to purchase entire commentary sets, such as The New International Commentary on the Old Testament (NICOT); The New International Commentary on the New Testament (NICNT); Word Biblical Commentary (WBC); Pillar New Testament Commentary; Baker Commentary; or Concordia Commentary, I advise purchasing commentaries individually by author. John Glynn's *Commentary & Reference Survey*, and bestcommentaries.com are my "go-to" recommendations for conservative, evangelical commentaries by author.[1]

10. **Stay in the Word and prayer yourself.** Prioritize and schedule personal time in God's Word and prayer. Have your secretary block it out. Hang a "Do Not Disturb" sign on your office door, and do not confuse sermon preparation with God time. Pour into your own cistern, lest you run dry from constant ministry demand. Jesus's invitation embraces ministers too: "If anyone thirsts, let him come to Me and drink" (John 7:37). The

---

[1] John Glynn, *Commentary & Reference Survey* (Grand Rapids: Kregel Academic & Professional Publications, 2007); www.bestcommentaries.com.

apostles allowed themselves to get sidetracked by competing ministry needs, yet when they re-centered themselves in Word and prayer—and delegated and empowered the rest—the church flourished (Acts 6:1-7). Come to think of it, perhaps we should move this point to the top of the list.

CHAPTER 12

Creative Expository Preaching: Sermons and Sermon Series

One area of expository preaching remains significantly underdeveloped: creative expository preaching. Google "creative expository preaching." Search a seminary's library database for "creative expository preaching." Now, tally your combined "hits." How many resources do you have?[1]

Unfortunately, some homiletical circles believe that *creative* and *expository preaching* do not belong together, almost like trying to mix water and oil: "Lest the pulpit succumb to a performance or show, let the preacher stick to the text, the whole text, and nothing but the text. So help him (or judge him), God." However, does *expositional*—even in Scripture—mean "lackluster," "monotonous," "tiresome," or "predictable"? Quite the contrary! In Matthew 25, Jesus could have stopped His exhortation at verse 13: "Watch therefore, for you know neither the day nor the hour." Instead, Jesus continues His exposition with a lengthy story: "For it will be like a man going on a journey, who called his servants and entrusted to them his property. To the one he gave five talents … " (Matt 25:14-30). To put it succinctly, when we consider (1) biblical example; (2) freedom in and with the gospel; (3) God's gift of human creativity; and (4) the promptings of the Holy Spirit as He illumines the text, can anyone credibly disdain creative

---

[1] I know of only one resource, and it is new to the field: Tony Evans, *The Power of Preaching: Crafting a Creative Expository Sermon* (Chicago: Moody Publishers, 2019).

expository preaching? After all, the sum of expository preaching yields to one overarching norm: *regardless of the sermon's wrapping, does it expound the text's intended meaning and purpose in a Christ-centered, redemptive way?* If the answer is *yes*, then the preacher can rest assured that he has rightly handled the Word of truth (2 Tim 2:15).

Below are two of my most creative expository sermons. The text for the first sermon is John 3:16, and the text for the second sermon is Philippians 2:3-8. Both sermons were preached on Christmas Eves.

Sermon One – John 3:16
"Heaven's Perfect Poker Match"

Scene 1: Satan

Intended function of the text and sermon: *That hearers would believe in God's only Son—His greatest token of love—and receive eternal life in Him.*

[Before the service begins, each worshipper receives a poker chip as he or she enters the sanctuary. In the chancel area I have a card table with two chairs and visible stacks of poker chips set up. One time I even had a small fogger machine to "emulate clouds of heaven," but not until the sermon started. Anyways, during the pre-sermon song, I go to a side-room and "dress like Satan"—red shawl, horns, and a plastic red pitchfork (easy on and easy off). Following the song, scene one commences when I walk out as Satan and say:]

Happy holidays—I love that one. It's so politically correct and tolerant. Am I glad that you're here tonight. You're about to witness the biggest poker game ever played. The stakes are high: God and I are playing for your eternal possession (pointing the pitchfork at the people). So, you might want to pay attention to this one. Game on!!! (Satan takes his seat at the poker table).

(Satan shuffles the deck of cards and says:) "God, would you like to cut? What's a matter, don't you trust me?" (Satan looking at his hand of cards) "Oh, this is gonna be good. (Showing the audience my hand and whispering to them) Three of a kind = 666. And these chips, look at all these chips. They're all on the table tonight. Each chip represents a sin. So many chips. So many sins. And they keep sinning. The chips keep piling up. Stack upon stack. Just look at all these chips, God. In fact, let's just take a minute and go through some of them." (I have ten stacks—one for each commandment).

Taking stack one: "Every time they don't put You first, God. What do we have here? Gods such as money, belongings, entertainment, medicine ... looking to all these things for help and happiness in life, but not to You. That's idolatry, and that means another chip!"

Taking stack two: "Wow, look at how many times they've taken Your name in vain: swearing in the locker room, out with friends, gaming, perverted jokes with buddies. What evil tongues they have ... (turning to congregants) Psssst: we speak the same language!"

Taking stack three: "Worship, let's talk about worship. We'll start with their attendance records: let's see ... Christmas Eve ... Easter. Christmas Eve ... Easter. Apparently there are only two weekends a year? God, let's face it. You don't matter ... only two weeks a year? You must understand though. Time is short. They're busy with work and play and friends and family. There's just no time for Sabbath rest."

Taking stack four: "Honor your father and mother. Look at their disobedience. All those times they've said "no" to mom or dad ... and evil thoughts about mom and dad too; dissing parents in front of friends; rolling eyes at them. Look at these chips."

Taking stack five: "Murder. Your word says that hate is the same as murder (cf. 1 John 3:15)! Harboring ill feelings toward family, in-laws, co-workers, church members, Illinois drivers, and government officials ... are we? (pause) Guilty!"

Taking stack six: "That brings us to adultery. Let's check their web-browser history: (pause) down and dirty! I see some porn, adult videos, sexting, lusting over other spouses, and cohabitation. And I know, let's take an abstinence before marriage poll!" (laughing: Ha! Ha! Ha! Ha! Ha!)

Taking stack seven: "Stealing. Oh, oh, oh, a number just came to mind: 1040! Cutting a couple of corners on taxes? Dishonesty at work? Fibbing about sick days? Those sudden coughs are such a pain, aren't they? Checking personal emails and texting on company time? More chips."

Taking stack eight: "God, if You haven't noticed ... liars! I wonder who they got that from? Okay, so they speak my native tongue: lying to parents, spouses, employers, friends, teachers, government, pastors ... not to mention slander, gossip, put downs... That's another nice stack of sins you got there."

Taking stacks nine and ten: "Coveting. These poor people, they need bigger homes, luxury cars, new 4K TVs, someone else's spouse, the latest gaming system and phone. Hey, it's the holiday season. You deserve it. You're even entitled to it. Go ahead, swipe, splurge, and enjoy!"

"God, do You see these chips? If they sin just 3x per day and live to be 70, that's more than 76,000 chips at just three sins per day; we both know that they sin A LOT more than that! And You know what a Righteous Judge must do. You can't ignore them. You can't just sweep their chips under a rug and forget about them. You can't just turn Your head to them. Each chip is a serious sin!"

(Satan raising his voice even louder) "And God, You know what Your Law says, 'The soul that sins is the soul that shall die.' And 'Those who practice sexual immorality, idolatry, sorcery, strife, jealousy, fits of anger, envy, drunkenness, murder, orgies and the like WILL NOT INHERIT THE KINGDOM OF GOD!' God, do You know what this means? (Shouting) God, do you know what this means? (Satan slams both hands down on the table so that stacks of chips fall ... then pause a few seconds) Their own sins condemn them. (Pointing to the people) They're mine! They're all mine! (Pointing the pitchfork at the people) Guilty as charged! I'm sorry God, but they're *ALL* coming with me!" (Pause a few seconds. Then Satan slowly stands up and walks off. The congregation sings a Christmas song during which I remove the red items and put on a white robe, crown, and scepter to represent God.)

Scene 2: God

(John 3:16 is also printed out in the bulletin underneath the heading for Scene 2).

(God walks out and sits on the other side of the card table. He picks up where Satan left off and speaks in a bold voice:) "I know what My Word says. I know that under My just and holy Law every one of them is guilty. Every day they do so many sins that hurt and offend Me."

(Pause) "Yet still, I love them. I made each of them with My hands. Every one of them is here because I planned them. That's why before I even created this world, I knew what I was going to do: I'm going ALL-IN!" (God reaches down and puts a cross up on the table.)

"I will give My Son, My only Son. He will come as a babe in Bethlehem. He will walk among them and perfectly obey My Law for them, and My Son will die in their place. He will be wounded for their transgressions, crushed for their iniquities ... by His stripes they will be healed. Their punishment that will be on My Son will bring them peace with Me. I will take every one of their sins, every single chip, and lay it on Him."

"My Word has another promise too, that every one of them, no matter who they are or where they've been or what they've done or how long they've been there ... WHOEVER believes in My

Son, in His perfect death and resurrection, will not perish but have eternal life. I will freely offer every one of them My most precious gifts: complete forgiveness for every sin and eternal life with Me." (Pause)

"Look at that, Satan, (God holding up His poker hand), the King of kings has a Royal Flush, and through faith in My Son, all of their chips have been taken off the table" (in one motion God sweeps all the chips off the table, leaving only the cross). (God saying boldly) "What accusations do you have against My people now? Huh? You lose!!! (Turning to the side and pointing). Michael, cast this serpent out of My presence for good!"

(God stands up and places himself at the center of the chancel facing the congregants.) As you came in this evening, hopefully you received one of these (hold up a poker chip). Carry this home with you. Keep it in your purse, your car, on your nightstand … remember what this night is all about. The God who loves you so much, that He went all-in with Jesus to win you back. You've heard His promise tonight: whoever of you believes in Jesus as your Lord and Savior will not perish but have the free gift of eternal life. Merry Christmas. Amen.

If you would like to know more about Jesus, or you have something that we could pray for this evening, we'd love to talk with you more after the service. Please stay and speak with me or seek one of our elders in the blue vests. We also have a Discovery Class and new sermon series on "Explore God" starting in January (or something similar to this post-script).

Sermon Two – Philippians 2:3-8
"The God Who Limbo-ed For You" (with an Alternate Ending)

Intended function of text and sermon: *Looking to Jesus and His profound humility from the cradle to the cross, that hearers would "limbo" for the people around them too.*

(At the start of the sermon I played "Limbo Rock" from Disney's "The Little Mermaid." While the song was playing, I had a wooden limbo bar with several notches set up in the chancel area, and I began with these questions:) Have you ever tried to limbo—even just for fun? Maybe as a child? Or with high school or college friends? Or with children or grandchildren? If so, how low could you go? A few feet? What if we lined up around the sanctuary and tried it tonight? What do you think: how low could you go? (pause while "Limbo Rock" fades to silence)

What do you think the Guinness World Record is for the limbo? Believe it or not, it's held by a young woman right here in Buffalo, New York. Shemika Campbell has set three Guinness records, including the record for the lowest limbo. Watch this video clip.[2] 8.5 inches! That's low. How many of you pulled a muscle or two just watching her? How low could you go?

A few years back, something struck me as I was reading the First Testament: from the very beginning, the Bible is directional. What do I mean by "the Bible is directional?" Listen to this:

- It says in Genesis 11:5, "The LORD came down (*yarad*) to see the city and the tower."
- God says in Genesis 18:21, "I will go down to see (the outcry of sin for Myself)."
- God assures Jacob in Genesis 46:4, "I Myself will go down with you to Egypt."

---

2 "Getting Low with the World Record Limbo Queen," Twisted Sifter, May 30, 2018, accessed July 1, 2018, https://twistedsifter.com/videos/getting-low-with-the-world-record-limbo-queen.

- In Exodus 3:8, God tells Moses from the burning bush, "I have come down to deliver them (the Israelites)."
- After God leads His people out of Egypt through the Red Sea, He says in Exodus 19:11, "And be ready for the third day. For on the third day the LORD will come down on Mount Sinai in the sight of all the people."
- God says in Numbers 11:17, "And I will come down and talk with you there (at the Tent of Meeting)."
- David records in 2 Samuel 22:10 how the LORD came down and delivered him from his enemies, including a giant with 12 fingers and 12 toes!
- Psalms, Isaiah, and Micah follow suit: "The LORD came down."

Some seventeen times in the First Testament we're told that God *came down*.[3] So already in Genesis, the Bible sets up the question: "How low would God go? How far would God come down for His people? How low would God go … for us?" Paul says in Philippians today: "Have this mind among yourselves, which is yours in Christ Jesus, who, though He was in the form of God, did not count equality with God a thing to be grasped, but made Himself nothing, taking the form of a servant, being born in the likeness of men" (Phil 2:5-7). Friends in Christ, how low would God go for you and for me? (Pause) The answer: (Pause) ALL THE WAY!

(Walk over to the limbo bar in the chancel area and lower it.) The eternal God of the universe came down and took on a frail, human body. The Nicene Creed declares it: "Who for us men and for our salvation *came down* from heaven and was incarnate by the Holy Spirit of the Virgin Mary and was made man." That's low: God willingly left His heavenly abode for a dirty cave or stall. God traded the brilliance and glory of heaven for the darkness of a Bethlehem sky. God left the praise of saints and angels to hear "moo, neigh, bah, bah, bah." (I know there's no biblical evidence

---

[3] The Hebrew verb *yarad* "to come down" or "to go down" appears in every aforementioned text.

for specific animals other than the feeding trough or manger. I merely did this for common Christmas effect.) God really knows how to limbo, doesn't He? (Long pause)

This limbo-talk reminds me of a Southwest commercial. An elderly man is pictured on a curbside feeding a flock of pigeons with seed. Suddenly, a sleek Porsche convertible honks and peels into the parking space where the gentleman is feeding the birds, and they flutter away. The narrator says, "That's low." After a break for Southwest lingo, the scene reopens with the elderly man tossing bird seed on the Porsche. The driver returns to a white-washed convertible and the narrator says, "That's lower."

Bethlehem is low … a helpless babe, but we have a God who goes even lower.

- Jesus welcomed the little children and babies who were brought to Him, catching rebuke from His disciples. (Lower the limbo bar another notch)
- Jesus reclined at a table with sinners and tax collectors, catching the rebuke of Pharisees and the religious leaders of His day. (Lower the limbo bar another notch)
- Jesus knelt down and came to the defense of a woman who'd been caught in adultery and about to be stoned to death. Jesus not only saved her life, He saved this woman's soul. (Lower the limbo bar another notch)
- The King of kings made His way to Jerusalem on a colt, the foal of a donkey. (Lower the limbo bar another notch)
- In an upper room, the God of the universe got down on His knees and washed the feet of His disciples. (Lower the limbo bar yet another notch)

How low would this God keep going for you and for me? Our text continues: "And being found in human form, He humbled Himself by becoming obedient to the point of death, even death on a cross" (Phil 2:8). (Lower the limbo bar all the way to the bottom). How low would God go to get us back? How low would Jesus go to save us from sin and an eternity in hell, an eternity of separation from God? Jesus went as low as one could possibly go—to the cross of Calvary. That's low (pointing to a manger). That's lower (pointing to the cross). Why? Because God in His unfailing love for you would rather give His own Son up on a cross than to have to live for eternity without us. (Long pause)

Ending A (aligns with the intention of the text): What about you? Following this kind of Savior, how low would you go? Paul exhorts us: "In humility count others more significant than yourselves. Let each of you look not only to his own interests, but also to the interests of others. Have this mind of Christ Jesus among you." So how low will you go? How low will you and I go to emulate Jesus in this world? While this world shouts: "You've got to go up in life. More money. More seniority. More degrees behind your name. Climb the corporate ladder. Go higher and higher." Jesus says, Jesus models, "My kingdom is about going down. I want you to go low for your neighbors." (Pause) How low will you and I go?

(Pointing to the cross) Jesus set the bar pretty low, didn't He? As we follow Jesus, how low are we willing to go this evening? How low are we willing to go as we look to the interests of neighbors and coworkers? Of family and in-laws? Of friends or fellow church members? How can you go low this week? (Close with a story or example of someone perhaps in the congregation or in your own life—who gave witness to Jesus by going low for someone else). Following the God who limbo-ed for us this evening, we go in His salvation and strength ... and we limbo for others too. Now go ... and be low. Amen.

Alternate Ending B (emphasizes biblical theology): And you know what? God's not done. Remember, our God loves to limbo. It's in His nature. It's who He is. And so, this God still comes down. He comes to us in His Word. He comes to us in His Supper. And more than anything, He wants to come down and declare residency in your heart.

Do you believe that? Do you believe that Jesus humbled Himself and paid for every sin on the cross? And do you believe that He rose again to offer you life? Have you been baptized into His name? If you have, then more than anything else this Christmas, He has already come down and made His home in you (pointing to the heart). If you haven't been baptized or you do not yet believe, but you want to hear more about Jesus, please let us know after the service. We'd love to continue this conversation with you. (Pause)

Oh, and remember who God is. He loves to limbo ... meaning He's not done yet. God has one grand limbo yet to come. Philippians 2 says that not only did Jesus rise from the dead and ascend to heavenly glory, but one day, He's coming back. He's coming down, in all His glory, to take us to His eternal home. And the Bible says that on that Day, every human being ever, believer and unbeliever, will bow low—all the way down—and confess that Jesus Christ is Lord. And that, my friends, is what this day, what Christmas is all about; it's about the God who would go as low as it would take to get you and me back so that He could live with us forever. Merry Christmas. Amen.

Sermon Series with Synopsis

In this section I share five of my favorite sermon series with you. I enjoy crafting sermon series because of the week-to-week connection between the texts and the theme—much like contemporary dramas on TV, Amazon, and Netflix. In addition, because the pastor can shape the series to the spiritual needs of the flock, he can target increased biblical understanding and worldview in specific areas and doctrines. Even if you preach the lectionary, you can still craft sermon series with a little bit of foresight and planning, especially when the lectionary works through a minor prophet, an epistle, or a large section of a gospel.[4]

---

[4] Though the Revised Common Lectionary (RCL) follows the life and ministry of Jesus, which is always good, the RCL "[Sundays and Special Days, not Daily] contains approximately 13 percent of the Bible—6 percent of the Old Testament (not counting the Psalms) and 41 percent of the New [Testament]." See Robert P. Waznak, *An Introduction to the Homily* (Collegeville, MN: Liturgical Press, 1998), 75. If congregants only hear preaching from the three-year lectionary, more than 85 percent of the Bible is never covered in the pulpit!

To that end, here is a sample of sermon series by biblical book, topic, church calendar, and an inspiring Christian author.

Book of the Bible
"Colossians: Life Under the Lordship of Christ"

Week 1: 1:1-14 "Your Reputation Precedes You"
- Commend the congregation as Paul commends Colossae for their faith in Christ and love for the saints. Give specific examples of fruitful works in Christ and where you have seen an increase in the knowledge of God.

Week 2: 1:15-23 "The Cosmic Christ"
- Exalt the cosmic, eternal magnitude of Jesus Christ—the Majesty who also stoops to reconcile and make peace by the blood of His cross in order that we would be holy, blameless, and above reproach in Him.

Week 3: 1:24-2:5 "A Purpose Driven Ministry"
- Paul suffers all to steward the gospel and proclaim Christ in order that he can present everyone mature in Christ on the Last Day. We toil in all His energy and power in the same purpose-driven ministry today.

Week 4: 2:6-23 "A Lesson in Self-Defense"
- Because of your sure standing in Christ and all that you have in Him, do not let anyone take you captive by deceitful teaching, philosophy, or false claims. Christ has disarmed and put them all to shame.

Week 5: 3:1-14 "A Whole New Wardrobe"
- If you've been buried with Christ in baptism and raised to new life in Him, then remove any dirty clothing and old ways and boldly sport your new apparel in Christ (i.e., your *Holy-ster*).

Week 6: 3:15-17 "More of the 'New You'"
- The "new you" includes the peace of Christ, thanks-living, preoccupation with the Word, and doing everything in Christ's name.

Week 7: 3:18-4:1 "The Christian Home"
- Reflect the Lordship of Christ in marriage, parenting, and childhood.

Week 8: 4:2-18 "Missional Living"
- Pray for doors to open through which the gospel of Christ can be proclaimed, which includes tempering our conduct and words because we represent Christ to the outside world.

Stewardship Series
"How to Be Rich" 1 Timothy 6:17-19. Inspired by Andy Stanley's *How to Be Rich*.[5]

Week 1: 6:17a "We're Rich"
- Let's face it, by God's grace we're materially rich in America, yet far richer in Christ. Hence, Paul speaks as much to us today as he did to the wealthy Christians in Ephesus.

Week 2: 6:17b-c "Holders Beware"
- Paul commands wealthy Christians in this age not to be haughty or to set their hopes on the uncertainty of riches, but to set their hope on the God who richly provides us with everything to enjoy. Christ is the only appropriate and reliable object of our hope!

Week 3: 6:18 "Being Good at Being Rich"
- Paul now exhorts wealthy Christians to do good, to be rich in good works, to be generous, and to be ready to share. As the redeemed of God, it is not what we have in life but what we do with what we have received. Christian generosity powerfully points people to the cross and to God's unfathomable riches in Christ.

Week 4: 6:19 "Investing for Eternity"
- Paul calls Christians to adopt a long-term investment approach because we have another world coming when Jesus returns. In fact, as a result of our baptismal union with Christ, Christian generosity lays up lasting treasure in heaven (cf. Jesus's words in Luke 12:33; 18:22).

---

5 Andy Stanley, *How to Be Rich: It's Not What You Have. It's What You Do with What You Have* (Grand Rapids: Zondervan, 2013).

Advent Series
"Home for the Holidays"

Week 1: Matthew 1:1-17 "Some Family Tree"
- As we consider going home for the holidays, I share some of the dysfunction in my family tree and in Jesus's, but He came to save us (1:21) so that we could be grafted by grace into His family tree.

Week 2: Luke 1:5-25 "Home Hurts"
- Sometimes home hurts by nature, by nurture, or by both. Zechariah and Elizabeth hurt, yet they still trust in God's goodness and walk obediently with Him.

Week 3: Luke 2:8-20 "Fond Memories"
- Home is also a place of fond memories. I briefly share some fond pictures and memories from my life up on the screen. Ultimately, however, I share pictures on the screen from what Mary's photo album might have looked like as I retell the story of Jesus from Bethlehem to His ascension.

Week 4: John 14:1-3 "A New Home"
- Jesus came so He could open wide His Father's home to all who believe in Him, and one day—any day—He's coming back to take us to our permanent abode.

Lenten Series
"The Road to the Final Four"
(This series coincides with March Madness & leads up to THE Final Four in Jesus's life: Maundy Thursday, Good Friday, Holy Saturday, and Easter Sunday)

Week 1: Luke 3:21-22 "Tip Off"
- Just as the road to the Final Four starts with a tip off, Jesus's baptism (and ours) marks the tip off on His road to THE Final Four.

Week 2: Luke 6:12-16 "Recruiting a Team"
- After Jesus's tip off, He recruits a team with some surprising picks. From eternity, Jesus recruited us to be on His team too—

all to the praise of His glorious grace.

Palm Sunday: Mark 11:1-11 "Passionate Fans"
- Who doesn't like a celebration? However, passionate fans can quickly abandon their fan-dom. In 2018, how many fans jumped on the UMBC wagon? How many of those fans follow UMBC today? How much more with Jesus then and now!

Maundy Thursday: Matthew 26:17-29 "Team Dinners"
- I remember team dinners in football and soccer. On this special night, Jesus provides His team with a supper—His broken body and poured blood for the forgiveness of sins. At this "team dinner" we enjoy intimate fellowship with Him and with our teammates—the one body of Christ.

Good Friday: Hebrews 9:11-26 "Leaving It All on the Court"
- Reaching the Final Four requires that teams "leave it all on the court." I showed a few bloody pictures on the screen from NCAA basketball. Jesus left it all on the court (the cross) for us—especially His blood (I showed a bloody picture of Him on the cross). Moreover, His loss … His sacrifice … is our victory and win.

Easter Sunday: John 20:1-18 "God's Slam Dunk"
- I showed three slam dunk videos that came up short and missed. When have we come up short too? On Easter morning, Jesus's followers thought that He had come up short, but He shows Himself risen! In addition, I paid for an internet picture of Jesus hanging on a basketball rim following a slam dunk, and I explained how Jesus hanging from the rim is picture of Him "throwing it down" over sin, death, and the devil on Easter morning. I concluded with three resulting applications for our lives.

Family Series

"Keeping a House or Building a Christian Home? Six Biblical Guidelines" (This series was personal because our family had just relocated to Chicagoland and purchased a house in the community.)

Week 1: Matthew 7:24-27 "The Foundation: Only One Will Last"

- Both builders face similar storms, but only one house stands. The storm—Judgement Day—is coming, and only homes that are built on Jesus and His Word will stand. God's grace allows rebuilds—even empowers them—and each new day is more time to build.

Week 2: Ephesians 4:15, 29-30 "Communication: Christian Maturity Includes the Tongue"
- As His children, God cares about the matter (truth) and manner (in love) of our communication with each another. In Christ our tongues can dispense grace and build up, rather than tear down and grieve the Holy Spirit.

Week 3: Ephesians 4:31-32 "Forgiveness: Taking Out the Trash Daily"
- Regardless of what trash (sins) has piled up in our homes, or how long we've been holding onto some of them, by the grace of God that has already forgiven us freely and fully, we can take our sins with one another to His dump (the cross) and leave them there.

Week 4: John 15:12-13 "Commitment: Family Mortar"
- Love (or commitment) to one another includes our closest neighbors—our immediate families, especially commitment to the marriage, to each family member, and the resolve with Christ to endure.

Week 5: Ruth 1:1-9, 14-18 "Surviving Storms" (preached on Mother's Day)
- Though storms hit every household, Ruth testifies to the hidden yet unfailing providence of God. God is constantly working (even in storms) to produce not what I want, but the me that He wants. Thus, in faith we "let go" and trust God's redemptive plan.

Week 6: Genesis 18:1-8 "Welcoming Homes"
- Abraham welcomes his guests, prepares a lavish feast for them, and even waits on them. However, when God visits homes (Abraham's and ours) He comes not to be blessed but to bless, just as Jesus blessed the homes of Levi, Martha, and Zacchaeus. Knowing Jesus through eyes of faith, we joyfully open our homes to this Guest. "Come, Lord Jesus, be our Guest, and let our homes by You be blessed. Amen."

CHAPTER 13

Why Expository Preaching Matters: A Final Encouragement

In 2016, *ABC News* aired a story about an eight-year-old boy in Illinois who was still breastfeeding.¹ The mom insisted, "Kyle is my only son and he's very important to me ... and he's going to be allowed to nurse until he decides to finish weaning himself."² Although critics accused her of serving her own needs rather than her son's, she maintains, "It's not about your needs, it's about putting your child first."³

Today's church faces a similar dilemma. At times, the church seems inundated with "nursing Christians." Men and women, some of whom have been professing believers for years, appear content with spiritual milk. The Second Testament actually reveals that "nursing Christians" have been in the church for two thousand years. The writers of Hebrews confront their intended audience:

> About this *we* (plural authors) have much to say, and it is hard to explain, since you have become dull of hearing. For though by

---

1 "Mom Still Breast-Feeds 8-Year-old Son," ABC News, July 9, 2016, accessed August 26, 2016, http://abcnews.go.com/GMA/story?id=125961&page=1. Though this weblink is no longer available, the story can still be accessed at https://www.nwitimes.com/uncategorized/mother-once-targeted-by-state-still-breastfeeds--year-old/article_4d484696-332c-54aa-8aa2-3db778551beb.html.

2 Ibid.

3 Ibid.

this time you ought to be teachers, you need someone to teach you again the basic principles of the oracles of God. You need milk, not solid food, for everyone who lives on milk is unskilled in the word of righteousness, since he is a child. But solid food is for the mature. (Heb 5:12-14)

The authors file a grievance with Hebrew Christians over their lack of spiritual maturity; they remain sucklings—underdeveloped in their walk with Christ and therefore not ready for the "solid food" of God's Word. Paul vents the same frustration with the church in Corinth: "But I, brothers, could not address you as spiritual people, but as people of the flesh, as infants in Christ. I fed you with milk, not solid food, for you were not ready for it. And even now you are not yet ready, for you are still of the flesh" (1 Cor 3:1-3a).

That God earnestly desires the growth and maturity of His body— the church—is no secret. Paul exhorts the Ephesians: "Rather, speaking the truth in love, we are to *grow up* in every way into Him who is the head, into Christ, from whom the whole body, joined and held together by every joint with which it is equipped, when each part is working properly, makes the body grow so that it builds itself up in love" (Eph 4:15-16). Likewise, Peter closes his second epistle, "You therefore, beloved, knowing this beforehand, take care that you are not carried away with the error of lawless people and lose your own stability. But *grow* in the grace and knowledge of our Lord and Savior Jesus Christ" (2 Pet 3:17-18a).

To that end, God commands the systematic preaching and teaching of His Word. Not only does expository preaching strengthen and nourish believers in Christ, but it fends off spiritual malnutrition too. Besides, God does not just commission His church to preach the Word (2 Tim 4:2), He blazes the homiletical trail before her.[4] From the onset of Jesus's public ministry, He "began to preach (khru/ssw), saying, 'Repent, for the kingdom of heaven is at hand'" (Matt 4:17). Similarly, Jesus instructs the Twelve the first time He sends them out: "Go rather to the lost sheep of the house of Israel. And preach (khru/ssw) as you go,

---

[4] The *Theological Dictionary of the New Testament* says of kerussō (to preach): "It means 'to cry out loud, declare, announce'... A general sense is 'to make known,' though specifically it may also mean 'to herald.'" Gerhard Kittel and Gerhard Fredrich, eds., *The Theological Dictionary of the New Testament*, abridged into one vol. by Geoffrey W. Bromiley (Grand Rapids: William B. Eerdmans Publishing Company, 1985), 432.

saying, 'The kingdom of heaven is at hand'" (Matt 10:6-7). Likewise, Jesus commissions His church through the apostle Paul:

> Preach (kerussō) the word, be ready in season and out of season; reprove, rebuke, and exhort, with complete patience and teaching. For the time is coming when people will not endure sound teaching, but having itching ears they will accumulate for themselves teachers to suit their own passions, and will turn away from listening to the truth and wander off into myths. (2 Tim 4:2-4)

By God's grace and design, preaching remains the non-negotiable privilege and responsibility of His church—the very means through which Jesus works to gather, strengthen, lead, and sustain His dearly purchased flock.

Modern expositors follow Jesus's lead and continue to underscore the necessity of expositional preaching. Timothy Keller says, "A careful expository sermon makes it easier for the hearers to recognize that the authority rests not in the speaker's opinions or reasoning but in God, in his revelation through the text itself... Expository preaching enables God to set the agenda for your Christian community."[5] John Stott even attributes the decline of Western churches to lackluster preaching and a loss of confidence in the gospel: "Now there is no chance of a recovery of preaching without a prior recovery of conviction. We need to regain our confidence in the truth, relevance and power of the gospel, and begin to get excited about it again. Is the gospel good news from God, or not?"[6] Stott concludes, "So, if the Church is to flourish again, there is no greater need than a recovery of faithful, powerful, biblical preaching."[7] Stott therefore challenges preachers: "It is our responsibility to teach them with clarity and conviction the plain truths of Scripture, in order to help them develop a Christian mind, and to encourage them to think with it about the great problems of the day,

---

5 Timothy Keller, *Preaching: Communicating Faith in an Age of Skepticism* (New York: Viking, 2015), 36.

6 John R. W. Stott, *Between Two Worlds: The Challenge of Preaching Today* (Grand Rapids: William B. Eerdmans Publishing Company, 1982), 85.

7 Ibid., 116.

and so to grow into maturity in Christ."[8]

Bryan Chapell and John MacArthur utilize a "shepherding image" to accentuate expository preaching and its indispensability to modern-day Christianity. Chapell states, "Preaching a sermon is an act of shepherding that requires a minister to consider every aspect of genuine structure, exegesis, and delivery as a potential tool for spiritual nurture, admonition, and healing."[9] MacArthur even cautions clergy: "Anything less than a commitment to expository preaching by the preacher will reduce his sheep to a weak, vulnerable, and shepherdless flock."[10]

Indeed, all Christian preaching should be expository in nature. That God has graciously given the church His Word in writing leaves no excuse for sheep to be underfed or infantile in faith. The cure for "church hunger" and "spiritual malnutrition" begins in the pulpit. Preach the gospel. Preach Christ expositionally from all Scripture.

> Jesus is THE Gift.
> The Gospel is the packaging.
> Preaching is the delivery truck.
> God's beloved are the address,
> And we are His ordained delivery guys.

We have His Spirit. We have His Word. We have His divine commissioning. Armed therefore with the gospel of Jesus Christ, God's backing, and the power of His indwelling Spirit, the anonymous brother in Corinth can define us all: "We are sending the brother who is famous among all the churches *for his preaching of the gospel ...* for the glory of the Lord Himself." (2 Cor 8:18-19). To that end: step up, step back, step out, step forward, and give yourself fully to the *prayer-infused, Christ-centered interpretation and proclamation of a passage's intended meaning and purpose, which gives rise to Spirit-empowered application and implication in the lives of hearers today.* My friend, boldly proclaim. In His might and for His glory. Amen.

---

[8] Ibid., 173.

[9] Bryan Chapell, *Christ-Centered Preaching: Redeeming the Expository Sermon*, 2nd ed. (Grand Rapids: Baker Academic, 2005), 85.

[10] John F. MacArthur and Masters Seminary Faculty, *Rediscovering Expository Preaching* (Dallas: Word Publishing, 1992), xvii.

From morning till evening he (Paul) *expounded* to them
testifying to the kingdom of God
and trying to convince them about Jesus
both from the Law of Moses and from the Prophets.
–Acts 28:23b

APPENDIX A

Joshua 1:1-9
"Facing Life's Transitions"

Intended Function of the Text and Sermon: *That the hearers would be strong and bold as they follow Jesus (The Greater Joshua) through life's many transitions to THE Promised Land.* (Written for the congregation that was transitioning between me and the pastor coming after me.)

Everyone faces transitions in life. Transitions can be positive or negative; transitions can be planned or blind-siding. I have listed some common transitions on the screen. *Retirement*: many think of retirement as a season in life when one can finally step back and enjoy the fruit of one's labors, yet retirement can be stressful. A person can devote him or herself to a career for several decades and suddenly find it finished, leaving the individual with an identity crisis, "Who am I apart from this job?" *New Parents* is also a transition in life; husband and wife are no longer just a couple, and the people around them begin to treat them differently too. For new parents, every day is a transition in itself. *Empty Nest*: I read about one couple whose youngest child left for college. After goodbyes, the husband went and sat down on the couch. His wife laid down on couch and rested her head on his lap. The husband reached down and gently removed her glasses. He said, "You know, dear, without your glasses you still look like the beautiful, young woman I married thirty years ago." "Honey," his wife replied, "without my glasses, you still look pretty good too." Other common transitions in life include *Divorce*; *Blended Families*; *In Between Jobs*; *Health*; *Moving*; *College* and the fast-track to independence; *Significant Loss* such as a loved one or pet; or *Start/Stop Driving*—when children start driving and parents no longer ride in the car with them; parents can only commend them to God's care and angels. Or, an elderly person surrenders decades of driving privileges and forfeits his or her sense of independent mobility.

Life has its share of transitions, and whether positive or negative, planned or blind-siding, transitions are intensely emotional and often stressful. A synonym for *transition* is *change*, and every change has three stages: an ending, a time of transition, and a new beginning. The most challenging season of change is often the middle—the time of transition when anxiety heightens and feelings of fear, doubt, and uncertainty arise. Where is the Rozelle family now? In the middle. Where is Pastor N. (your next pastor) and his family now? In the middle. Where is Holy Cross now? In the middle, and the middle can be a big, hairy, and scary place to be. Where do you think God's people are in today's text? You guessed it, right in the center of transition, yet God's words to Joshua help us face life's transitions too.

Please look at verse 1 with me. "After the death of Moses the servant of the LORD, the LORD said to Joshua the son of Nun, Moses' assistant, 'Moses My servant is dead.'" By the way, who's the greatest orphan in the Bible? Joshua—the son of "Nun." (Pause) But what do you do when the first five books of the Bible end with a funeral? You can see the map of the area on the screen. Moses went up on Mount Nebo. The Israelites were used to Moses going up mountains to be with God for extended periods, only this time was different. Moses, their leader for forty years, did not come down. He died there on Mount Nebo, outside of the Promised Land. If you look at your notes, what amazes me is that God does not recall Moses' sins. In spite of his sin and failure, three times in our text today the LORD still refers to Moses as "My servant." God does not recount that He forbade Moses to enter the Promised Land because Moses struck the rock in the wilderness of Zin rather than speaking to the rock as God had commanded him (see Num 20:11). God in His grace only renders Moses: "My servant." Psalm 116:15 says, "Precious in the sight of the LORD is the death of His saints."

We continue with verse 2: "Moses My servant is dead. Now therefore arise, go over this Jordan, you and all this people." Crossing the Jordan River is a formidable command to Joshua. (Pause) We've lived in the greater Niagara Falls area for twelve years of ministry now. Like most attractions, when you live by one you only visit when company comes. What I remember most from our visits to Niagara Falls is this: long before you see the actual falls, you hear them. You hear the 750,000 gallons per second roaring over the edge, plummeting some 190' to the river below. My friends, what do we know about the Jordan River when God speaks these words to Joshua? If you look at the screen, you can see how the Jordan River normally flows about 80 to 100 feet wide ... mostly calm, isn't it? However, during flood stage in April, the Jordan River looks like this! (pictures on the screen of the Jordan River at flood stage) The raging Jordan overflows its banks and can be a mile-wide in places. We know from Joshua 3 that God commands Joshua to cross the Jordan River during flood stage when the river looks like this (pointing again to the screen). When God speaks this command to Joshua, we know that he can hear the power of the river in the background. Yet no obstacle is too big for our God! "Arise, cross this Jordan, you and the two to three million men, women, and children who are with you, plus your livestock and all of your goods, into the land I am giving you."

Once again, notice the primacy of grace in Scripture; God stresses "the land I am giving you." The Promised Land is a gift. The Israelites didn't earn it. The Israelites certainly don't deserve it. But God is the "Great Giver" and His people are but passive recipients of His grace. (Pause)

Look with me in verses 3 and 4 at the size of God's gift to Israel: "Every place that the sole of your foot will tread upon I have given to you, just as I promised to Moses. From the wilderness and this Lebanon as far as the great river, the river Euphrates, all the land of the Hittites to the Great Sea toward the going down of the sun shall be your territory." Why this land? You can see the extent of God's gift up on the screen. Of all the land that God could have chosen to give His people, why this land? What are the three principles of real estate? Location. Location. Location. Looking at the screen, note how this land serves as a strategic land bridge that connects three continents. This land also has a highway that connects the great Mesopotamian civilization and its Euphrates River in the North to the great Egyptian civilization and its Nile River in the South, meaning that over the centuries millions of travelers and traders would pass through this land. Considering its prime location, do you think God chose this land because of something He wanted to bring into it, or because God had something planned to go forth from it? In just 1,400 years, God's own Son would traverse this land; from this prime location, the good news of Jesus was set to go viral. (Pause)

Let's continue with God's words to Joshua in verses 5 and 6: "No man shall be able to stand before you all the days of your life. Just as I was with Moses, so I will be with you. I will not leave (literally *drop*) you or forsake you. Be strong and courageous (literally *be bold*), for you shall cause this people to inherit the land that I swore to their fathers to give them." God affirms that His people will face opposition, but with God it will come to naught. Even though the inhabitants of Canaan will not simply hand over their land to the invading Israelites, God assures Joshua that His purpose will prevail. This truth reminds us of Jesus's words: "In the world you will have tribulation. But take heart; I have overcome the world" (John 16:33). In Jesus, the oppositions we face eventually come to naught too.

Another important subtheme is woven throughout this passage: God always provides leadership for His people. God reassures His new leader: "Just as I was with Moses, so I will be with you." Joshua is not called to fill Moses' shoes; he is only called to fill the shoes that God has given him to fill. Some might say that the next pastor at Holy Cross has big shoes to fill, but depending on the make, I only wear a size nine. My shoes are not that big. And the next pastor does not have to fill my shoes—only the shoes that God has ordained him to fill.

"Just as I was with Moses, so I will be with you." God holds up His impeccable track record with Moses and promises Joshua His abiding presence too. By implication, God declares to Joshua:

> Just as I was with Moses in the burning bush; just as I was with Moses in the ten plagues; just as I was with Moses in the pillar of cloud by day and the pillar of fire by night; just as I was with Moses when the Israelites crossed the Red Sea on dry ground and the most powerful army on earth was drowned; just as Moses

tossed a log into the water and it became sweet to drink; just as I showed My glory through the manna on the ground and caused enough water to come from a rock to hydrate 2 to 3 million people plus their livestock ... so I will be with you.

God's promises do not die with Moses. He keeps every pledge; God never goes back on a single word. Through Joshua, God was about to deliver on His promise to Abraham, Isaac, and Jacob to give His people this good and gracious land.

In the Hebrew language God literally tells Joshua, "I will not drop you." The word for "drop" is used elsewhere in the Old Testament for hay *dropping down* into a burning fire; for a mighty one *dropping* his girdle; and for *dropping* one's hand. "I will not drop you," says God; our God does not fumble what He holds in the palm of His hands.

God also promises in the text, "Nor will I forsake you." The word "forsake" is used with walking out of a house or a city; it's also used of an animal forsaking its young. God promises that He will never walk out on Joshua. What God promised to never do to Moses or Joshua or to us, He did to His only Son. Remember Jesus's cry of dereliction: "My God, My God, why have You forsaken Me?" God turned His back on Jesus, so that He would never have to turn His back on any of us.

As Joshua is about to lead God's people into a new land with major obstacles and mighty armies, what's his confidence? What's his security in the unknown? We know what it isn't: it isn't Joshua's skills or years of experience under Moses. Nor is it his charisma or impressive resume. Rather, in the midst of this seismic transition, God's people rest in His unfailing presence. (Pause) Friends, isn't that the answer to all of life's transitions? Whether schooling, children, new work, loss of health, moving across the country or even world: in life's transitions—planned and unplanned—the final answer is always the unfailing presence of our God. Regardless of life's Doppler forecast, is anything more certain than an oath by the living God? *I will not drop you, nor will I forsake you.* (Pause)

Look how God continues His exhortation to Joshua in verses 7 and 8: "Only be strong and very courageous, being careful (literally *be very bold to keep/guard and*) to do according to all the law (*Torah*) which Moses My servant commanded you. Do not turn from it to the right or to the left, that you may have good success wherever you go. This Book of the Law (literally *Scroll of the Torah*) shall not depart from your mouth, but you shall meditate on it day and night, so that you may be careful to do according to all that is written in it. For then you will make your way prosperous, and then you will have good success." A life that is prosperous and successful in God's eyes does not deviate from His Word; in the Word there is great reward. In her book *Amazing Grace*, author and poet Kathleen Norris tells about Arlo, a rugged, self-made man who got married. For his wedding, Arlo's grandfather spared no expense and bought the newlyweds a leather-bound Bible with their names engraved in gold. Arlo and his wife thanked granddad for the thoughtful gift but later placed the unopened Bible in a closet. Sometime later, Arlo sought the Bible and opened it. He was shocked to find a twenty-dollar bill at the beginning of Genesis ... and another one at the beginning of Exodus ... and a crisp $20 bill at the beginning of every book. How many books are in the Bible? Sixty-six books ... times twenty dollars? Granddad placed over $1,300 in their Bible, wondering if the newlyweds would ever open it. Arlo and his wife had no idea of the great treasure that awaited inside their Bible; all the couple had to do was open it. The treasure was there.

Everything that Joshua needs for success is right there in the first five books of the Old Testament. Three times in the text God repeats the command to "be strong and be bold," but this is the only time when God adds "be strong and be *very* bold" *to keep and obey His Torah*, His teaching and instruction. A life in the Word effects obedience and great reward, but a life that ignores the Word bears disobedience and the consequences of human sin. In fact, if I could leave you with one thing at Holy Cross as you continue to move forward, it's this: hold fast to the Word! Scripture says in 2 Timothy 4:3-4, "The time is coming when people will not endure sound teaching, but having itching ears they will accumulate for themselves teachers to suit their own passions, and will turn away from listening to the truth and wander off into myths." Hold fast to the Word, for it is also this Word from Genesis to Revelation that points us to our Lord and Savior, Jesus Christ. Every time you open His Word, the greatest treasure awaits. (Pause)

Holy Cross, as we close this section with verse 9, notice God's assurances to Joshua once again: "Have I not commanded you? Be strong and courageous (literally *be bold*). Do not be frightened, and do not be dismayed, for the LORD your God is with you wherever you go." Do you see those other verse references on your sermon notes (3:7, 10; 4:14; 6:27; 10:14, 42; 13:6; 14:12; 21:44; 23:3, 10)? Guess what message God wants His people to know again and again throughout the book of Joshua? (Pause) I am with you! And Yahweh proved it as they crossed the raging Jordan on dry ground; as the walls of Jericho came tumbling down; as the sun stood still until Israel won in battle; and as they divided the Promised Land between the tribes of Israel ... just as God had promised.

We might think, "That's great for Joshua, but what about a plain Christian like me?" (Pause) God didn't just repeat the promise of His presence to you, He heightened it in Jesus! By God's grace we follow a new Joshua, an even greater Joshua. Guess what the Greek name for Joshua is? Jesus. Now guess what the Hebrew name is for Jesus? Joshua. Yet these servants of the Most High share more than names. (Pause) Where was Jesus commissioned? (Pause) Yah, the same place as Joshua: at the Jordan River. (Pause) And what was Jesus's mission? (Pause) To lead God's people into the Promised Land, but not before He fought the greatest enemies of all time—sin, Satan, and death—laying His very life down in the decisive battle. But three days later, Jesus stood upright again! The doors of Paradise, the ultimate Promised Land, flung wide-open to all who believe in Him.

And this God ... still promises you in His Son ... whatever transitions you face in life, do not be afraid. Do not be dismayed. I will not drop you. I will not forsake you—in life or in death. Be strong and be bold! I am Immanuel, God with you, and I will be with you wherever you go. In the name of the Father, and of the + Son, and of the Holy Spirit. Amen.

APPENDIX B

Luke 19:1-10
"So Others May Live"

Intended Function of Text and Sermon: *In the face of declining churches, that the Gospel would embolden hearers in mission with Jesus to seek and to save the lost.*

The most recent stats on the Lutheran Church—Missouri Synod reported the following: In 2010, 54% of LC-MS congregations reported no adult confirmations; 65% of LC-MS congregations reported confirming 1 adult or less; and 80% of LC-MS congregations confirmed 3 adults or less. From 1997 to 2012, the US population grew 17% from 268 million to 314 million citizens. During that same period, the LC-MS lost 325,000 members—a 15% decline. Since the 1970s, the LC-MS continues to lose more than 20,000 members each year; if we continue at the current rate, within 90 years the LC-MS will cease to exist. My grandchildren and great-grandchildren will witness the end of our Missouri Synod. (Pause)

In our own Erie and Niagara Counties of Western New York, the 2010 census reported that 1.2 million people live in our counties. Nearly half of those polled in our own backyard—45.3% or 514,314 people—claim *no* religious affiliation at all … more than half a million religious "nones." And while Christianity is down in Buffalo-Niagara by more than 300,000 souls in the past 10 years, Mormonism is up

42% and Islam is up a staggering 242% in the same region. In fact, for the first time there are more Muslims (18,483) in our counties than Missouri-Synod Lutherans (16,964).

If you could state how you are feeling right now, what would it be? Shell-shocked? Dazed and confused? Saddened? Depressed? Disoriented? Stirred? Upset? Disheartened? Spiritually numb? The question becomes, "What do we do? What do we, the body of Christ ... the church on earth ... do in this state of decline? Where do we go from here?" (Pause)

Let's go back to Jesus. Let's go back to Jesus and His mission; let's go back to why He came here in the first place. Jesus has the answer we desperately seek. He recalibrates our focus. Jesus realigns our mission with His mission, and His Spirit empowers and invigorates us to carry out His purposes in this world.

Perhaps nowhere is the mission of Jesus more clearly seen in Scripture than in our text from Luke 19:1-10. Luke records (author's translation),

> Jesus entered Jericho and was passing through. And behold, there was a man named Zacchaeus. He was a chief tax collector and was rich. And he was seeking to see who Jesus was, but on account of the crowd he could not, because he was small in stature. So he ran on ahead and climbed up into a sycamore tree to see Him, for He was about to pass that way. And when Jesus came to the place, He looked up and said to him, "Zacchaeus, hurry and come down, for I must stay at your house today." So he hurried and came down and received Him joyfully. And when they saw it, they all grumbled, "He has gone in to be the guest of a man who is a sinner." And Zacchaeus stood and said to the Lord, "Behold, Lord, the half of my goods I give to the poor. And if I have defrauded anyone of anything, I restore it fourfold." And Jesus said to him, "Today salvation has come to this house, since he also is a son of Abraham. For the Son of Man came to seek and to save the lost." (Pause)

Would you pray with me? Lord Jesus, "Let the words of my mouth and the meditation of my heart be acceptable in Your sight, O LORD, my Rock and my Redeemer (Ps 19:14). Amen."

We begin with verse 1: "Jesus entered Jericho and was passing through." This section of Scripture actually begins in Luke 9:51 when Jesus "sets His face to go to Jerusalem" and is termed the "travel narrative" (Luke 9:51–19:27). In these chapters of Luke, Jesus makes His way toward Jerusalem, His destination city as Messiah. If you look at the map on the video screen you can see that Jericho sits about 17 miles to the east of Jerusalem. Hence, Jesus is simply passing through. However, He does not leave Jericho without two powerful demonstrations of God's grace. Immediately before our text—while still on the outskirts of Jericho—Jesus heals a blind man who cries out to Him for mercy. And now, as Jesus enters Jericho, He changes the life (and eternity) of a man called Zacchaeus.

We continue with verses 2 and 3. "And behold, there was a man who was called Zacchaeus; he was a chief tax collector, and he was rich. And he was seeking to see who Jesus was, but he was not able on account of the crowd, for he was small in stature." The text gives us quite a bit of information about Zacchaeus. First, we're told that he's a chief tax collector. Jericho was a well-known toll place in Palestine, especially for goods passing east and west between Judea and Perea. A chief tax collector had other toll collectors under his authority, and together they received tolls and tariffs on goods. The sticky point with Roman taxation was this: the chief tax collector had to pay the Romans the expected tax revenues from his region in advance. The chief tax collector would then inflate the local tax rate to recover what he had already paid the Romans, plus make a profit. As you can imagine, the entire toll system was open to abuse and dishonesty, especially since only tax collectors knew the Roman tax rate. Given the prosperity of the region at the time, as well as his occupation as chief tax collector, there's no wonder the text tells us that Zacchaeus is rich. He's made a nice living for himself on the commission he's taken from other people. In other words, Luke gives us a good whiff of the first-century IRS!

However, the text informs us that this man of big financial stature is lacking in another "measure." How can I say this politically correct? Zacchaeus is vertically challenged! He's a short stack! In fact, the Greek New Testament literally reads, "a little one in height"; "little one" is where we get our English word *micro* from. The dude's tiny, and with the crowds pressing around Jesus, his small stature proves a "tall obstacle" for him ... no pun intended. Zacchaeus can't see over the crowds to get a good look at Jesus. Why Zacchaeus wants to see Jesus, we're not told, but like other well-known figures in society, he likely heard reports about Jesus and hopes to get a glimpse of the prophet, rabbi, and miracle worker from Nazareth too. (Pause)

Our text continues in verse 4: "So Zacchaeus ran on ahead and climbed up into a sycamore tree to see Him, for He was about to pass that way." The New Testament (Herodian) Jericho had numerous parks and avenues in which trees grew, and if you look at the screen, I have a picture of a sycamore tree for you. These trees stand about 30 to 40 feet tall. Notice their short trunks and spreading branches, very ideal for holding a grown man. What jumps out in this verse is Zacchaeus' running and climbing. For a Palestinian man in his position to run in public and climb a tree was extreme and uncharacteristic—even undignified behavior—yet the opportunity to behold Jesus of Nazareth motivates Zacchaeus to cast aside all social and cultural norms and do whatever it takes to see Jesus as He passes by. What happens next is incredible.

Verse 5 states, "And when Jesus came to that place, He looked up and said to him, 'Zacchaeus, hurry and come down, for I must stay at your house today.'" Jesus pulls three shocking moves here. First, when He arrives at the tree where Zacchaeus is perched, it's Jesus who looks up at Zacchaeus. Second, Jesus calls the tax collector by name! We're not told how Jesus knows his name; it could simply be Jesus's divine knowledge as the Son of God. Third, Jesus invites Himself to stay at Zacchaeus's house! Jesus breaks with social norms too. Doesn't a person normally wait to be invited to someone else's house, or at least make a polite request? Not Jesus, His words communicate divine necessity, practically a command: "Zacchaeus, I must stay at your house today!" What's Luke highlighting here? (Pause) Who is seeking whom? Is Zacchaeus the one seeking to see Jesus, or is Jesus the One seeking Zacchaeus? (Pause) How will Zacchaeus respond to Jesus's request? I mean, forget the need to take a selfie from the tree, Jesus just invited Himself to hang at Z's house!

Look at Zacchaeus's response in verse 6: "So Zacchaeus hurried and came down and received Him joyfully." Zacchaeus does exactly what Jesus says; he hurries and comes down. In fact, Zacchaeus comes down so fast it almost sounds as if he fell out of the tree. Zacchaeus can't earn Jesus's company. Zacchaeus doesn't deserve Jesus's company; all he can do is receive this Guest with joy. Zacchaeus doesn't just get a glimpse of Jesus from a tree, he—of all people—gets to host Jesus in his very home, and he welcomes Jesus with great joy.

Notice in verse 7 how Luke shifts to the response of the crowd as they watch this scene unfold. "And when they saw it, they all grumbled, 'He has gone in to be the guest of a man who is a sinner.'" The symbolic nature of Jesus's stay with Zacchaeus is obvious to everyone. The crowd praises Jesus's miracle in chapter 18, but they take issue with the person He befriends in chapter 19. Jesus doesn't choose to stay at the house of a priest or ruler or notorious disciple. He chooses the house of a known sinner, and Luke lets us know that everyone grumbles about it. Jesus pulls the shock factor yet again. Of all the houses in Jericho to choose from, Zacchaeus's goes against every expectation for a rabbi of Jesus's stature. (Pause)

We often do the same thing, don't we? We grumble and make armchair assessments of who does and who does not matter to God; therefore, God must not have any use for them in His kingdom either. Yet here we see Jesus in mission, surrounding Himself with the undesirable, the unconvinced, the spiritually confused, the morally bankrupt people of the town, people we often look at and keep our heads high too. (Pause) I have a crisp $20 bill in my hand. How many of you would take this $20 bill? You bet! You could take someone to the movies, go to lunch, buy some gas or groceries with it. It's a genuine $20 bill. (I fold the bill in half.) Alright, how many of you would take this $20 now? Look, it has a crease right down the middle. (I fold the $20 bill several more times.) How many of you would take it now? (I tear part of the $20 bill.) How about now? Would you still take it? (Finally, I take the $20 bill and wad it up into a tiny ball, drop it on the floor, and jump up and down on it several times so that it's a *micro* green ball.) How many of you would still take this $20 bill? Why? Why would you still take it? It's not nice and crisp anymore; it's a complete mess. There's no way it would feed into an automated checkout lane. Why would you still want it? (Wait for someone to give the answer: because it's still worth $20!) That's right, no matter what this bill looks like, no matter how bad it's messed up, it still retains its full value as a $20 bill! And that's how Jesus sees people—including Zacchaeus. No matter what people have done or how many times they've done it. No matter where people have been or how long they've been there. No matter how they appear to us on the outside or on the inside, they still retain their full value as human beings created in God's image, and His kingdom is as open to them as it is to anyone!

And our text suggests something more. Not only does it say that Jesus entered Zacchaeus's house, it reveals that Jesus had table fellowship with him. Dining with someone in first-century Palestine communicated full acceptance and friendship; plus, receiving hospitality from Zacchaeus bestowed honor on him as the host. Jesus's acts of lodging with a sinful publican and dining with him declare nothing less than God's full and unconditional acceptance of this known sinner. At its core, this story magnifies the amazing and unbelievable grace of God in Jesus Christ!

We're told now in verse 8 that Zacchaeus is so moved by God's grace in Jesus, that he stands and says, "Behold, Lord, the half of my goods I give to the poor. And if I have defrauded anyone of anything, I restore it fourfold." A changed heart, a heart that has been touched by Jesus, is evidenced by a changed life. Old Testament passages such as Leviticus 6:5 and Numbers 5:6-7 speak of repaying people who've been wronged the full amount plus an additional 20%; Zacchaeus vows a 400% return. Not only that, Zacchaeus pledges half of his goods to the poor. Jesus accepts sinners as they are, but He never leaves them as they are. His grace changes people from the inside out. Zacchaeus's encounter with Jesus immediately changes the way he handles his money and possessions—from taking advantage of others to serving their needs. His actions evidence his faith and conversion, his genuine repentance and the good works that always follow faith.

And look at how Jesus affirms the genuineness of Zacchaeus' faith in verse 9: "And Jesus said to him, 'Today salvation has come to this house, since he also is a son of Abraham.'" Jesus affirms that salvation has come to Zacchaeus's house, and Jesus identifies Zacchaeus, a sinful outcast among outcasts, as a true son of Abraham. Just as the Bible declares Abraham righteous by his faith in the LORD (Gen 15:6), Zacchaeus shares the same faith as father Abraham did. And if Zacchaeus is a son of Abraham by faith, then he's also an heir of God's promises in heaven (Rom 4:3, 9, 22; Gal 3:6, 29; Jas 2:23)! And so are you, by faith in the God of Abraham and Zacchaeus! By God's grace in Jesus Christ, Zacchaeus is an example of a rich man whose wealth does not prevent him from entering the kingdom of heaven. By God's grace in Jesus Christ, Zacchaeus is an example of a rich man who passes through the eye of a needle (Luke 18:24-27).

Yet the climax of this story, as well as of the entire travel narrative that began 10 chapters prior, unfolds in verse 10. Jesus explains this encounter with Zacchaeus in one short phrase: "For the Son of Man came to seek and to save the lost." If there's a quest in Luke 19, it's not Zacchaeus's desire to see Jesus, it's Jesus's quest to seek and to save the lost tax collector. Zacchaeus was lost in the sin of his wealth and corruption, yet Jesus takes the initiative to seek him out and bring salvation to his house. And note this: these words in verse 10 are not Luke's own commentary on the story; these words come right from Jesus's mouth. He defines His mission—His purpose as God in the flesh—as that of seeking and saving lost sinners. Through Jesus Christ, God is taking the initiative to seek out and fully receive even the vilest of sinners into His kingdom. Jesus is the Champion—the Savior—of sinful outcasts, including you and me.

(Pause)

Several years ago I enjoyed watching *The Guardian*; it's a movie about the heroic and sacrificial efforts of the US Coast Guard. The bonus menu on the DVD features live interviews from four Coast Guard rescue swimmers; please look at the screen. (Play DVD Bonus Features: "Unsung Heroes" 00:02:32—00:05:32 on the video screen.) What's the Coast Guard Rescue Swimmer's motto? "So Others May Live." How much more the mission of Jesus and His church: "So Others May Live." *For the Son of Man came to seek and to save the lost.* By the end of Luke 19, Jesus reaches His destination that began in Luke 9; He rides into Jerusalem on a donkey. And by chapter 23, Jesus dies on a cross, but not before He reaches out to one more outcast, a condemned criminal on a cross beside Him. Yet to this unworthy criminal Jesus boldly proclaims, "Truly, I say to you, today you will be with Me in Paradise."[1] Moments later, Jesus breathes His last breath. Even His final act on the cross is defined by reaching out, by seeking and saving one

---

1 Luke 23:43.

more lost person for eternity. (Pause)

Three days later, Jesus rises again. He's alive. He won, and to this day He's still on the loose in this world seeking and saving lost sinners. By His grace, and only His grace, He sought and found us too. And He has called us and commissioned us as His Church to partner with Him in His mission: "So Others May Live." That's Jesus's answer to where do we go from here. By His grace ... and in the power of His Spirit, we go. We take the good news of this Champion and Friend of sinners—and summoned by Jesus to join Him on God's rescue mission—we go. Amen.

APPENDIX C

Sample Sermon Notes

"Facing Life's Transitions"
Joshua 1:1-9

Transitions in life can be positive or negative, planned or blindsided, but either way, they are intensely _____ and often _____. A synonym is _____.

Vs. 1-2) After the death of Moses the servant of the LORD, the LORD said to Joshua the son of Nun, Moses' assistant, "Moses My servant is dead. Now therefore arise, cross this Jordan, you and all this people, into the land that I am giving to them, to the people of Israel."

- God doesn't recall Moses' _____! (Ps 116:15)
- God's promises don't _____ with Moses.
- The primacy _____ "land I am giving to them" for God!

Vs. 3-4) Every place the sole of your foot will tread upon I have given to you, just as I promised to Moses. From the wilderness and this Lebanon as far as the great river, the river Euphrates, all the land of the Hittites to the Great Sea toward the going down of the sun shall be your territory.

- Why this land? _____ (3x)!!!!

Vs. 5-6) No man shall be able to stand before you all the days of your life. Just as I was with Moses, so I will be with you. I will not "drop" you or forsake you. Be strong and be bold, for you shall cause this people to inherit the land that I swore to their fathers to give them.

- God affirms that His people will face _____ but with God it will _____. (Jn 16)
- Subtheme: God always provides _____ for His people.
- God holds up His impeccable _____!
- What promised to never do to Moses or Joshua or us, He did _____! (Mark 15:34)
- The final answer to life's _____ is His presence.

Vs. 7-8) Only be strong and be very bold to keep and to do according to all the Torah which Moses My servant commanded you. Do not turn from it to the right or to the left, that you may have good success wherever you go. This Scroll of the Torah shall not depart from your mouth, but you shall meditate on it day and night, so that you may be careful to do according to all that is written in it. For then you will make your way prosperous, and then you will have good success.

- A life that is prosperous and successful in God's eyes is one that does not _____ from His Word!

Luther, "Scripture calls ruminating accepting God's Word with real earnestness, taking it to heart, loving it, and finding delight in it, diligently considering it, and holding fast to it."

- A life in the Word produces both _____ and great reward, and vise-a-versa!!!
- Holy Cross, _____! (1 Tim 4:1; 2 Tim 4:2-4)

Vs. 9) Have I not commanded you? Be strong and be bold. Do not be frightened, and do not be dismayed, for the LORD your God is with you wherever you go. (2:24; 3:7, 10; 4:14; 6:27; 10:14, 42; 13:6; 14:12; 21:44, 23:3, 10)

- What about a "plain Christian" like me? God didn't just repeat this promise to you, He _____ (Emmanuel "God with us").

APPENDIX D

Recommended Resources

Step Up
Accordance by OakTree Software, Inc., or *Logos Bible Software* by Faithlife

Step Back
Carson, D. A., Douglas J. Moo, and Leon Morris. *An Introduction to the New Testament*. 2nd ed. Grand Rapids: Zondervan Publishing House, 2005.

Dillard, Raymond B., and Tremper Longman III. *An Introduction to the Old Testament*. 2nd ed. Grand Rapids: Zondervan Publishing House, 2006.

Harris, R. Laird, Gleason L. Archer, Jr., and Bruce K. Waltke, eds. *Theological Wordbook of the Old Testament*. 2 vols. Chicago: Moody Press, 1980.

Kittel, Gerhard, and Gerhard Friedrich, trans. *The Theological Dictionary of the New Testament*. Abridged into one volume by Geoffrey W. Bromiley. Grand Rapids: William B. Eerdmans Publishing Company, 1985.

Paul, Ian, and David Wenham, *Preaching the New Testament*. Downers Grove, IL: IVP Academic, 2013.

Sandy, D. Brent, and Ronald L. Giese, Jr. *Cracking Old Testament Codes: A Guide to Interpreting the Literary Genres of the Old Testament*. Nashville: B & H Academic, 1995.

Schreiner, Thomas R. *Interpreting the Pauline Epistles*. 2nd ed. Grand Rapids: Baker Academic, 1990.

Wallace, Daniel B. *Greek Grammar Beyond the Basics: An Exegetical Syntax of the New Testament*. Grand Rapids: Zondervan Publishing House, 1996.

Step Out

Beale, G. K. *A New Testament Biblical Theology: The Transformation of the Old Testament in the New*. Grand Rapids: Baker Academic, 2011.

Goldsworthy, Graeme. *Preaching the Whole Bible as Christian Scripture: The Application of Biblical Theology to Expository Preaching*. Grand Rapids: William B. Eerdmans Publishing Company, 2000.
According to Plan: The Unfolding Revelation of God in the Bible. Downers Grove, IL: InterVarsity, 2002.

Greidanus, Sidney. *Preaching Christ from the Old Testament: A Contemporary Hermeneutical Method*. Grand Rapids: William B. Eerdmans Publishing Company, 1999.

Keller, Timothy. *Preaching: Communicating Faith in an Age of Skepticism*. New York: Viking, 2015.

Schreiner, Thomas R. *The King in His Beauty: A Biblical Theology of the Old and New Testaments*. Grand Rapids: Baker Academic, 2013.

Step Forward
Davis, Dale Ralph. *The Word Became Fresh: How to Preach from Old Testament Narrative Texts*. Fearn, Scotland: Mentor, 2012.

Stott, John R. W. *Between Two Worlds: The Challenge of Preaching Today*. Grand Rapids: William B. Eerdmans Publishing Company, 1982.

Illustrations
www.preachingtoday.com

Commentary Evaluation
John Glynn, *Commentary & Reference Survey* (Grand Rapids: Kregel Academic & Professional Publications, 2007).

BIBLIOGRAPHY

Adam, Peter. *Speaking God's Words: A Practical Theology of Preaching.* Vancouver: Regent College Publishing, 2004.

Adams, Jay E. "Editorial: Good Preaching Is Hard Work." *The Journal of Pastoral Practice* 4, no. 2 (1980): 1.

Bauer, Walter. *A Greek-English Lexicon of the New Testament and Other Early Christian Literature.* Revised and edited by Frederick William Danker. 3rd ed. Chicago: University of Chicago Press, 2000.

Beale, G. K. *A New Testament Biblical Theology: The Transformation of the Old Testament in the New.* Grand Rapids: Baker Academic, 2011.

Broadus, John A. *A Treatise on the Preparation and Delivery of Sermons.* 2nd ed. Philadelphia: Smith, English & Co., 1871.

Brown, Francis, S. R. Driver, and Charles A. Briggs. *The Brown-Driver-Briggs Hebrew and English Lexicon: With an Appendix Containing the Biblical Aramaic.* Peabody, MA: Hendrickson Publishers, 2000.

Bryson, Harold T. *Expository Preaching: The Art of Preaching through a Book of the Bible.* Nashville: Broadman & Holman Publishers, 1995.

Cahill, Dennis M. *The Shape of Preaching.* Grand Rapids: Baker Books, 2007.

Carson, D. A. *Exegetical Fallacies*. 2nd ed. Grand Rapids: Baker Books, 1996.

Carson, D. A., Douglas J. Moo, and Leon Morris. *An Introduction to the New Testament*. 2nd ed. Grand Rapids: Zondervan Publishing House, 2005.

Chapell, Bryan. *Christ-Centered Preaching: Redeeming the Expository Sermon*. 2nd ed. Grand Rapids: Baker Academic, 2005.

Craddock, Fred B. *As One without Authority*. Rev. ed. St. Louis: Chalice Press, 2001.

Davis, Dale Ralph. *The Word Became Fresh: How to Preach from Old Testament Narrative Texts*. Fearn, Scotland: Mentor, 2012.

Dillard, Raymond B., and Tremper Longman III. *An Introduction to the Old Testament*. 2nd ed. Grand Rapids: Zondervan Publishing House, 2006.

Doriani, Daniel M. *Putting the Truth to Work: The Theory and Practice of Biblical Application*. Phillipsburg, NJ: P & R Publishing, 2001.

Dumas, Dan, ed. *A Guide to Expository Ministry: Guide Book No. 003*. Louisville: SBTS Press, 2012.

Evans, Tony. *The Power of Preaching: Crafting a Creative Expository Sermon*. Chicago: Moody Publishers, 2019.

Fant, Clyde E., Jr. *20 Centuries of Great Preaching: An Encyclopedia of Preaching*. Vol. 2, *Luther to Massillon, 1483-1742*. Edited by William M. Pinson, Jr. Waco, TX: Word Books, 1971.

Fee, Gordon. *Paul's Letter to the Philippians*. NICNT. Grand Rapids: Eerdmans Publishing Company, 1995.

George, Timothy. *Reading Scripture with the Reformers*. Downers Grove, IL: IVP Academic, 2011.

Glynn, John. *Commentary & Reference Survey: A Comprehensive Guide to Biblical and Theological Resources*. Grand Rapids: Kregel Academic & Professional, 2007.

Goldsworthy, Graeme. *According to Plan: The Unfolding Revelation of God in the Bible*. Downers Grove, IL: InterVarsity, 2002.
Preaching the Whole Bible as Christian Scripture: The Application of Biblical Theology to Expository Preaching. Grand Rapids: William B. Eerdmans Publishing Company, 2000.

Greidanus, Sidney. *Preaching Christ from the Old Testament: A Contemporary Hermeneutical Method*. Grand Rapids: William B. Eerdmans Publishing Company, 1999.

Harris, R. Laird, Gleason L. Archer, Jr., and Bruce K. Waltke, eds. *Theological Wordbook of the Old Testament*. 2 vols. Chicago: Moody Press, 1980.

Heisler, Greg. *Spirit-Led Preaching: The Holy Spirit's Role in Sermon Preparation and Delivery*. Nashville: B & H Academic, 2007.

Helm, David R. *Expositional Preaching: How We Speak God's Word Today*. Wheaton, IL: Crossway, 2014.

Kaiser, Walter C. *Toward an Exegetical Theology: Biblical Exegesis for Preaching & Teaching*. Grand Rapids: Baker Academic, 1981.

Kaiser, Walter C., and Moises Silva. *An Introduction to Biblical Hermeneutics: The Search for Meaning*. Grand Rapids: Zondervan Publishing House, 1994.

Keller, Timothy. *Preaching: Communicating Faith in an Age of Skepticism*. New York: Viking, 2015.

Kittel, Gerhard, and Gerhard Friedrich, trans. *The Theological Dictionary of the New Testament*. Abridged into one volume by Geoffrey W. Bromiley. Grand Rapids: William B. Eerdmans Publishing Company, 1985.

Kolb, Robert, and Timothy J. Wengert, eds. *The Book of Concord: The Confessions of the Evangelical Lutheran Church*. Minneapolis: Fortress Press, 2000.

Kurvilla, Abraham. *A Vision for Preaching: Understanding the Heart of Pastoral Ministry*. Grand Rapids: Baker Academic, 2015.

Lawrence, Michael. *Biblical Theology in the Life of the Church: A Guide for Ministry*. Wheaton, IL: Crossway, 2010.

Lischer, Richard, ed. *The Company of Preachers: Wisdom on Preaching, Augustine to the Present*. Grand Rapids: William B. Eerdmans Publishing Company, 2002.

Lloyd-Jones, D. Martyn. *Preaching & Preachers*. 40th anniversary ed. Grand Rapids: Zondervan, 2011.

MacArthur, John F., and Masters Seminary Faculty. *Rediscovering Expository Preaching*. Dallas: Word Publishing, 1992.

MacPherson, Ian. *The Art of Illustrating Sermons*. Nashville: Abingdon, 1964.

Mohler, R. Albert, Jr. *He Is Not Silent: Preaching in a Postmodern World*. Chicago: Moody Publishers, 2008.

Olford, Stephen F., and David L. Olford. *Anointed Expository Preaching*. Nashville: Broadman & Holman Publishers, 1998.

Paul, Ian, and David Wenham, eds. *Preaching the New Testament*. Downers Grove, IL: IVP Academic, 2013.

Plass, Ewald M., comp. *What Luther Says: A Practical in-Home Anthology for Active Christians*. St. Louis: Concordia Publishing House, 1959.

Richard, Ramesh. *Preparing Expository Sermons: A Seven-Step Method for Biblical Preaching*. Grand Rapids: Baker Books, 2001.

Roberts, Vaughan. *God's Big Picture: Tracing the Storyline of the Bible.* Downers Grove, IL: IVP Books, 2002.

Robinson, Haddon W. *Biblical Preaching: The Development and Delivery of Expository Messages.* 3rd ed. Grand Rapids: Baker Academic, 2014.

Sandy, D. Brent, and Ronald L. Giese, Jr. *Cracking Old Testament Codes: A Guide to Interpreting the Literary Genres of the Old Testament.* Nashville: B & H Academic, 1995.

Schreiner, Thomas R. *Interpreting the Pauline Epistles.* 2nd ed. Grand Rapids: Baker Academic, 1990.
The King in His Beauty: A Biblical Theology of the Old and New Testaments. Grand Rapids: Baker Academic, 2013.

Spurgeon, Charles H. *Lectures to My Students.* Grand Rapids: Baker Book House, 1977 [1894].
The Quotable Spurgeon. Wheaton, IL: Harold Shaw, 1990.

Stanley, Andy. *How to Be Rich: It's Not What You Have, It's What You Do with What You Have.* Grand Rapids: Zondervan, 2013.

Stott, John R. W. *Between Two Worlds: The Challenge of Preaching Today.* Grand Rapids: William B. Eerdmans Publishing Company, 1982.

Vines, Jerry, and Jim Shaddix. *Power in the Pulpit: How to Prepare and Deliver Expository Sermons.* Chicago: Moody Press, 1999.

Voelz, James W. *What Does This Mean? Principles of Biblical Interpretation in the Post-Modern World.* 2nd ed. St. Louis: CPH, 1997.

Wallace, Daniel B. *Greek Grammar Beyond the Basics: An Exegetical Syntax of the New Testament.* Grand Rapids: Zondervan Publishing House, 1996.

Waltke, Bruce K., and M. O'Connor. *An Introduction to Biblical Hebrew Syntax*. Winona Lake, Indiana: Eisenbrauns, 1990.

Waznak, Robert P. *An Introduction to the Homily*. Collegeville, MN: Liturgical Press, 1998.

Wiggins, Grant, and Jay McTighe. *Understanding by Design*. 2nd ed. Alexandria, VA: Association for Supervision and Curriculum Development, 2005.

Willhite, Keith. *Preaching with Relevance without Dumbing Down*. Grand Rapids: Kregel Publications, 2001.

Willimon, William H., and Richard Lischer, eds. *Concise Encyclopedia of Preaching*. Louisville: Westminster John Knox Press, 1995.

York, Hershael W., and Bert Decker. *Preaching with Bold Assurance: A Solid and Enduring Approach to Engaging Exposition*. Nashville: B & H Publishing Group, 2003.

www.ingramcontent.com/pod-product-compliance
Lightning Source LLC
Chambersburg PA
CBHW070550170426
43201CB00012B/1790